DEEPER DEVOTIONALS

ANSWERING
the CALL of
Jesus
the MASTER
40-DAY DEVOTIONAL

Chara Hoseinee-Friday

ANSWERING the CALL of JESUS the MASTER

Copyright © 2019 by Chara Hoseinee-Friday

Printed in the United States of America

First Printing, 2019

ISBN: 9781091809499

Imprint: Independently published

DEDICATION

To all who are hungry for the truth of salvation.
You shall know it and be made eternally free.
John 8:32

To all believers desirous of intentionally living
the abundant life made available to us through
the grace of Jesus Christ. You shall have it in
abundance to the fullest, till it overflows.
John 10:10

ACKNOWLEDGEMENTS

I GIVE HONOUR TO GOD the Father, JESUS CHRIST the Son and our Redeemer and the blessed HOLY SPIRIT whose words I have been privileged to pen in this work. It is by His continuous counsel and distinct instructions through my own spiritual journey that I have learnt the principles documented in ANSWERING THE CALL OF JESUS THE MASTER and I am able to share with you.

I especially thank you, my beloved husband and best friend, Sean Friday. Your unconditional love, encouragement and support inspire me to continually pursue God's perfection in my life. Thank you for always seeing my potential in the now and never allowing me to give up on my dreams. I love you.

To my wonderful family, thank you for continued love and support. You all have been my inner circle of strength and the pillars of truth that I can always depend upon. To my dearest and closest friends, thanks for your unwavering support and helping me stay grounded. To my beloved Couva Revival Centre family and Pastors, Bishop Lew Thomson and Lady Joy Thomson, thank you for your continued prayers, love, encouragement and the opportunity to grow and develop as an individual and in ministry.

I love you all.

CONTENTS

Day I
Follow Me

Mark 1:16–20 (Amplified Bible)

[16]As Jesus was walking by the shore of the Sea of Galilee, He saw Simon [Peter] and Simon's brother, Andrew, casting a net in the sea; for they were fishermen. [17]And Jesus said to them, "Follow Me [as My disciples, accepting Me as your Master and Teacher and walking the same path of life that I walk], and I will make you fishers of men." [18]Immediately they left their nets and followed Him [becoming His disciples, believing and trusting in Him and following His example]. [19]Going on a little farther, He saw James the son of Zebedee, and his brother John, who were also in the boat mending and cleaning the nets. [20]Immediately Jesus called to them; and they left their father Zebedee in the boat with the hired workers, and went away to follow Him [becoming His disciples, believing and trusting in Him and following His example].

*I*T SEEMED LIKE A typical day by the Sea of Galilee for these four men; Simon and Andrew, along with James and John. These two sets of brothers came as always to ply their trade as fishermen. They were engrossed in their routine tasks as one pair was casting their net and the other, mending and cleaning. Everything appeared normal and predictable but, life as they knew it was about to be changed forever by a predestined encounter with Jesus, the Master. As the Son appeared on the horizon and approached them with purposeful strides, He uttered a simple instruction, *"...Follow Me and I will make you fishers of men."* (Mark 1:17 King James Version)

I've often wondered what would have been my response to this clear yet peculiar instruction/invitation that resembled more of a command. Would I have left the career I built and countless hours invested; my family and friends and followed this compelling stranger, no questions asked? Would I have discerned that He was no ordinary man, and I was highly favoured by God to share in His life, teachings, and experiences? Would I have submitted my spirit to be touched by His divinity, humbly casting the net of my will aside and enthusiastically shouted *"Yes!"* to this new Master that pointedly addressed me?

All believers in Jesus Christ were once like these men, engrossed in executing our self-serving agendas because it was all that we knew to do. Then one day, His call pierced through the chaos in our souls, awakening our spiritual awareness to our desperate need for a relationship and fellowship with God the Father. But accepting His call necessitates that we completely submit and surrender our will to God's, wholly embracing His divine plan and purpose for our lives. From the outside looking in, that may seem like a tall order because it requires us to let go, everything.

> **"But accepting His call necessitates that we completely submit and surrender our will to God's, wholly embracing His divine plan and purpose for our lives."**

We can certainly attest that many of the demands being made on our oversubscribed schedules were non-existent as recent as a few years ago and non-issues for our forefathers. Modern devices, entertainment and social media portals generated by our rapidly advancing technology and the world's insatiable thrust towards leisurely de-stressors ensnare our attention daily, deceptively enticing us into nouveau self-gratification. While the methods have evolved the desired end persists; that our fleshly desires be appeased gradually undermining our spiritual tenacity. Being sufficiently distracted, we may find ourselves becoming more and more detached in fellowshipping with God as our intimacy fades away in tandem with our spiritual connectivity with Him.

If after you've read the introductory paragraphs of this Devotional, you realize a gap is emerging between your commitment and His call to service, don't despair. We've all had lapses in judgment, including myself, and lost sight of His call along the way. Even His very disciples were at times captivated by matters that diverted their attention from the Truth that walked amongst them. Inherently, there is nothing wrong with this discovery, it's actually charged with opportunities for empowerment. What you choose to do with this finding however, is crucial to fulfilling His call as our next steps could either stimulate spiritual growth or encourage stagnation. We must also remember that while we may have an impelling desire to obey the Master, we have an enemy whose snares and distractions are intent on smothering and deflecting our most earnest intentions. As such, let's not be deceived into believing there is no urgency in our need to refocus since apathy ensures that our regression gradually advances.

If you are committed to embarking on this journey with me over the next few weeks, then let us begin by refocusing on the Master's call and resolutely bring it centre stage. Let us be purposeful in the choices that we make each day by ensuring they align with His perfect plans. Also, let us intentionally pursue intimacy with the Divine Saviour by communing with the Holy Spirit and His awesome presence daily. As He speaks, let us hear His voice that guides us onto our path of purpose, receive His expressions of love towards us through His word and follow His instructions and direction.

Listen. Receive. Obey.

Let us determinedly choose to respond like His first disciples; Simon, Andrew, James and John fully trusting in Him as we leave our way to follow The Way.

> [5]Thomas said to Him, "Lord, we do not know where You are going; so how can we know the way?" [6]Jesus said to him, "I am the [only] Way [to God] and the [real] Truth and the [real] Life; no one comes to the Father but through Me.
> **John 14:5–6 (Amplified Bible)**

Day 40

Day 2
Going It Alone

Genesis 12:1–7 (The Message)

[1]God told Abram: "Leave your country, your family, and your father's home for a land that I will show you.

[2-3]I'll make you a great nation and bless you.

I'll make you famous; you'll be a blessing.

I'll bless those who bless you; those who curse you I'll curse. All the families of the Earth will be blessed through you."

[4]So Abram left just as God said, and Lot left with him. Abram was seventy-five years old when he left Haran.

Genesis 13:14–16 (Amplified Bible, Classic Edition)

[14]The Lord said to Abram, after Lot had left him, "Now lift up your eyes and look from the place where you are standing, northward and southward and eastward and westward; [15]for all the land which you see I will give to you and to your descendants forever. [16]I will make your descendants [as numerous] as the dust of the earth, so that if a man could count the [grains of] dust of the earth, then your descendants could also be counted.

*W*E GENERALLY don't like to go it alone. But as exemplified in the relationship with Lot and Abram, sometimes people move on just like the phases of life and many persons whom we once held close are no longer with us. We may also find that as our fellowship and intimacy with God deepened the significance of some relationships decreased wholly uninfluenced by malice or discrimination. Parting ways by a proverbial fork in the road of relationship is sometimes purely an eventuality of our response to humbly follow His plans for us. Nostalgia though, has an uncanny knack of instantaneously washing over us when we revisit scenes from our past and remember familiar faces that were present during the most significant moments in our lives.

While we can't help our humanness at times, we must, however, come to terms with certain realities. Separation is sometimes unavoidable when it becomes necessary to extract ourselves from the resident din of our familiar environments to hear Him. When we set ourselves apart, not necessarily reclusively, the clarity in His communication does not compete as much for our spirit's attention against the wealth of issues that impact us daily. Here, we wrestle less and less with our moral rectitude as we increasingly submit to the power of His presence. In the resultant quietness, His words can resonate deep within our spirit with clarity, fine-tuning the direction of His perfect will.

Abram's relationship and journey with God began when his father decided to leave his home in Ur of the Chaldeans with a handful of his immediate family members. He intended migrating to Canaan but, they settled in Harran where Terah eventually died thus beginning a new chapter in Abram's life (Genesis 11:27–32). God's instructions now flowed through personal interaction with Abram and, though obedient to the call to move, he followed the pattern of his earthly father as he also took along an entourage. Still, through his obedience, today all believers on the Lord Jesus Christ are perpetually blessed (Galatians 3:14–29). But what was the price he had to pay for us to inherit *"the blessings of Abraham"*, a term clichéd among believers today? Do we myopically focus primarily on its effect, or have we given any considerable thought with gratitude to its genesis?

To follow the call of God, Abram had to humbly embrace a nomadic lifestyle and make choices that would eventually strip him down to an almost kin-less existence having no family but his wife, Sarai at his side. Despite the noticeable physical limitations evidenced by their age and the arid plains that lay between him and his destination, he journeyed on in faith to the place that only God could show him to start a promised lineage without an heir.

> **❝When we obey God, we can never envisage the immense ripple effect wrapped up in that one action or quantify its spiritual returns.❞**

By his submission and obedience, God made a covenant with Abram that would span his generations validated when God changed his name from *"Exalted Father"* (Abram) to Abraham, *"Father of a Multitude"* (Genesis 17 Amplified Bible).

When we obey God, we can never envisage the immense ripple effect wrapped up in that one action or quantify its spiritual returns. As such, we could never know how our submission to God would affect those around us or how they would affect others, even from generation to generation. Like Abraham, the extent of our impact can be as multitudinous as the grains of sand. But what we do know is we can be confident that in our obedience God will bless us in ways and measures that transcends our foresight and comprehension. He will superabundantly exceed our expectations infinitely beyond our greatest prayers, hopes and dreams (Ephesians 3:20–21).

We already have what we need to make the journey from where we are to where God has predestined. There are no gaps in His strategy or lack of provision in His plan, so there is no need for timidity or fear regarding what lies ahead. Rest assured, with Him in us and us in Him (1 John 4:13) we can be confident about success because despite the lack of resources and physical companionship, we are never alone and by His grace, we will make it to our journey's end.

Have I not commanded you? Be strong and courageous!
Do not be terrified or dismayed (intimidated),
for the Lord your God is with you wherever you go."
Joshua 1:9 (Amplified Bible)

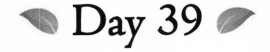

Day 39

Day 3
"Who? ME?"

Judges 6:11–16 (New King James Version)

¹²And the Angel of the Lord appeared to him, and said to him, "The Lord is with you, you mighty man of valour!"

¹³Gideon said to Him, "O my lord, if the Lord is with us, why then has all this happened to us? And where are all His miracles which our fathers told us about, saying, 'Did not the Lord bring us up from Egypt?' But now the Lord has forsaken us and delivered us into the hands of the Midianites."

¹⁴Then the Lord turned to him and said, "Go in this might of yours, and you shall save Israel from the hand of the Midianites. Have I not sent you?"

¹⁵So he said to Him, "O my Lord, how can I save Israel? Indeed my clan is the weakest in Manasseh, and I am the least in my father's house." ¹⁶And the Lord said to him, "Surely I will be with you, and you shall defeat the Midianites as one man."

*H*IS NAME MEANT Mighty Warrior. Since his birth, every time someone called Gideon by his name, they released this prophecy about him into the atmosphere that was yet to be revealed. But up to the time of his encounter with this celestial being, he could not appreciate or embrace what his name meant. He was unable to understand and grasp this declaration made about him. Instead, he dutifully narrated the reprise of limitations that he had come to accept about his feeble lineage and his insufficiencies that together, in his estimation, did not a *'Mighty Man of Valour'* make. After all, in his attempt to hide from the enemy and complete a task consequential to survival, he was found using a wine-press to thresh wheat.

The messenger from the Lord was neither perturbed nor perplexed by what Gideon believed about himself but addressed him as the man God created him to become, which in fact he already was. He looked at Gideon and saw the man in whom God entrusted all the qualities and the strength to deliver Israel out of the hands of those same Midianites he was presently hiding from. Although his initial response did not mirror the words spoken to him, by his pointed statements, he revealed that in his heart these very issues were of grave concern to him.

Amid his self-proclaimed ineptitude, he had questions churning deep within his spirit about the present state of his people and the notably absent hand of Jehovah, their covenant keeping God (Deuteronomy 7:9; Psalm 105:8). He felt that God lost sight of Israel's trouble and, blinded by his apparent abandonment issues it escaped him that it was, in fact, their covenant God who sought an audience with him. Gideon was now being commissioned as the catalyst to effectuate the deliverance they so desperately needed. The angel came specifically to outline his assignment to him, and he could not recognise it.

The answers to the burning questions in our hearts oftentimes do not come in the ways we expect or predict. There are instances when we embody the answers that we seek and to that reality we are just unaware, being engulfed primarily with the issues at hand. Taking on new challenges, or addressing these mammoth type situations without this knowledge, automatically one can accept that the preconceived assumption is correct: the task is too big, and I am too small. How could one so insignificant, so weak

> **❝He never sets us up to fail as victory is always the goal, placed supernaturally in our hands by the authority He has given us through Christ.❞**

and so ineffective take on the armies of the enemy while being completely preoccupied with simply trying to survive?

Throughout the scriptures God has established a pattern. He repeatedly uses those who are categorically weak, infirmed, outcast, downtrodden, and simple to be vessels for His power and the manifestation of His glory here on earth (1 Corinthians 1:28–29). He continuously proves to us that whomever He calls He also empowers by His Holy Spirit to do that very thing which is inconceivable, insurmountable and even impossible. God has called each of us to a specific purpose and path to fulfil His work. When the time comes for us to move into action, I can assure you that we will save ourselves time and avoid stress-related fear if we believe that He knows what He is doing, which He does. He never sets us up to fail as victory is always the goal, placed supernaturally in our hands by the authority He has given us through Christ.

As he addresses the potential personification of your present self, do not resist His call or be side-tracked by what you perceive you lack.   Furthermore, don't mistakenly and blindly believe that the voice of the people is the voice of God because Gideon proved them all wrong. While your mind churns away looking for solutions, take a minute to ponder on His words in your quiet moments and just say *"YES"*. That is all He needs to hear from our hearts and with our lips. Trust Him, and He will do the rest.

> [3]Strengthen the weak hands and make firm the feeble and tottering knees. [4]Say to those who are of a fearful and hasty heart, Be strong, fear not! Behold, your God will come with vengeance; with the recompense of God He will come and save you.
> **Isaiah 35:3–4 (Amplified Bible, Classic Edition)**

Day 38

Day 4
The Attitude Of No

Jonah 1:1–3, 12–14 (New King James Version)

[1]Now the word of the Lord came to Jonah the son of Amittai, saying, [2]"Arise, go to Nineveh, that great city, and cry out against it; for their wickedness has come up before Me." [3]But Jonah arose to flee to Tarshish from the presence of the Lord. He went down to Joppa, and found a ship going to Tarshish; so he paid the fare, and went down into it, to go with them to Tarshish from the presence of the Lord.

[12]And he said to them, "Pick me up and throw me into the sea; then the sea will become calm for you. For I know that this great tempest is because of me." [13]Nevertheless the men rowed hard to return to land, but they could not, for the sea continued to grow more tempestuous against them. [14]Therefore they cried out to the Lord and said, "We pray, O Lord, please do not let us perish for this man's life, and do not charge us with innocent blood; for You, O Lord, have done as it pleased You."

HAVE YOU EVER told God *"No!"*... by your actions? There aren't many people you would meet with the wherewithal and brazen-faced enough to actually say the word after receiving direct instructions from God. But how many times have we received a direct message from the Lord through His servant, His word or even had the witness in our spirit courtesy the blessed Holy Spirit and our initial response conveys the very word? Although we may lack the courage to open our mouths and speak it into the atmosphere, we seem to have the courage to think it in our hearts and display it in our behaviour. How so? By countering His instructions with any of the following responses: complacency, procrastination, apathy, unresponsiveness, laziness, and in this case, a complete and defiant U-turn.

It does not matter how much we try to hide from God in whatever way we think would work, seemingly legitimate to onlookers or not. Whether we busy ourselves with the administration of church work, run to and fro giving attention to charity cases or just spend our time concentrating on being the best Christian example that we can, we could still be missing the mark. Though these activities might seem very important in the greater scheme of things, we could be focusing in all the wrong areas and effectively, maybe even purposefully, sidestep the true calling of God. More than seeing what we do, He sees the motive behind our doings and hears the unspoken words resident in our hearts, so we can give up trying. There is no hiding from the presence of the Lord (Hebrews 4:13). Besides, although we may believe that evading His instruction frees us to do as we please and dodge the consequences, we will never be truly free until we obey.

> **"More than seeing what we do, He sees the motive behind our doings and hears the unspoken words resident in our hearts..."**

Furthermore, what about the people whose lives we place in jeopardy by our rebellion? The people we associate with while we continue dilly-dallying, wasting time and being disobedient may find themselves deeply affected by our fears, maybe even placed in harm's way. Let us also consider those who are continuing along the path of death and destruction, unaware that they are awaiting our obedience to intercept their imminent debacle. Moreover, we are not in any position to judge the sinner for sin because that was once our lot in life until we encountered the Master.

Jonah's disobedience subjected him to a most interesting form of transportation that ensured he reached Nineveh's shores. He knew that his rebellious actions were the cause of the tempestuous seas and the resultant fear that ravaged all the seafarers. They had an even greater fear of the solution that he offered to their calamity until they realised that there was truly no alternative. Now innocent spectators were pleading to God for mercy, trapped by a solution that only spelled murder as a result of Jonah's insolence. As Jonah accepted his fate unbeknownst to him, God provided the means, though unorthodox and grotesque, to take him to Nineveh where he found a people ready to repent of their sin. It is amazing how the message of truth can transform a nation from debauchery and destruction to restoration and reconciliation.

I encourage us all not to leave His call unattended or think it is inconsequential to do so. God has a panoramic view of everyone on the threshold of transformation that is dependent on our affirmative response, even the effects on us, and them, if we refuse our call. They are lost and in need of God's grace, and

He has selected us to be their witness of the gospel in their helplessness. Let's not make them, or God, wait one second longer; the time for our obedience is now! Let's endeavour to get it right the first time.

Samuel said,
"Has the Lord as great a delight in burnt offerings
and sacrifices as in obedience to the voice of the Lord?
Behold, to obey is better than sacrifice,
And to heed [is better] than the fat of rams.
1 Samuel 15:22 (Amplified Bible)

 # Day 37

Day 5
The Un-Veiling

Isaiah 6:1–8 (Amplified Bible)

[1]In the year that King Uzziah died, I saw [in a vision] the Lord sitting on a throne, high and exalted, with the train of His royal robe filling the [most holy part of the] temple.

[2]Above Him seraphim (heavenly beings) stood; each one had six wings: with two wings he covered his face, with two wings he covered his feet, and with two wings he flew.

[3]And one called out to another, saying, *"Holy, Holy, Holy is the Lord of hosts; The whole earth is filled with His glory."*

[4]And the foundations of the thresholds trembled at the voice of him who called out, and the temple was filling with smoke.

[5]Then I said, *"Woe is me! For I am ruined, Because I am a man of [ceremonially] unclean lips, And I live among a people of unclean lips; For my eyes have seen the King, the Lord of hosts."*

[6]Then one of the seraphim flew to me with a burning coal in his hand, which he had taken from the altar with tongs.

[7]He touched my mouth with it and said, *"Listen carefully, this has touched your lips; your wickedness [your sin, your injustice, your wrongdoing] is taken away and your sin atoned for and forgiven."*

[8]Then I heard the voice of the Lord, saying,

"Whom shall I send, and who will go for Us?" Then I said, *"Here am I. Send me!"*

*T*HERE ARE TIMES when each of us must take that moment and meditate on the very concept revealed to Isaiah in this unprecedented encounter with God. But are we truly prepared and equipped to identify the veils that impair our ability to see the Lord in His sovereignty, hear His voice with clarity and respond submissively? Realistically speaking just like our famed prophet, we may find ourselves struggling to identify those distractions and obstructions, especially the ones that are closest to us. It was only after the death of his beloved king that Isaiah saw himself beyond prophet status, called by God to servanthood.

I'm always amazed at how our ability to discern God's will and purpose for our lives makes the things we think are significant inconsequential. Somehow in God's presence and divine purpose, our once intense consciousness of their importance seems to diminish or even vanish! Could it be possible that the dethroning of these "monarchs"; those things in our lives we may have unconsciously become dependent upon for enablement and protection, awaken a greater desire for servanthood in us? Could they be contributors to some of the weight that entangles and distracts us from focusing on the race set before us (Hebrews 12:1–2)?

> **I'm always amazed at how our ability to discern God's will and purpose makes the things we think are significant inconsequential.**

Well, Isaiah's experience has shown us that God could turn everything around, changing the landscape of our clearly defined paths for ourselves in an instant. It is quite clear that his view of

God changed instantaneously when the reality of his vision sank in. He immediately lost sight of himself and even the title he carried as he was drawn into the presence of his Holy, Holy, Holy Lord; becoming an eye-witness to His glory, royalty and magnificence. As he beheld this heavenly scene, the only words he could utter constituted an all-out confession of his woeful uncleanness, lamenting the same of his people, to which the Lord responded with purification. Hereafter, it did not matter to Isaiah what the Lord was calling him to do, he was ready to serve and the words of affirmation and dedication to servanthood just rolled off his lips from his heart.

The request was a simple one, *"Whom shall I send ... who will go for Us?"* It is a request that He continues to make of all believers everywhere, redefined today in the great commission of the New Testament church of Jesus Christ (Mark 16:15; Matthew 28:19–20). In Isaiah's account, three words come to mind from his encounter with and response to God: awe, availability, and agreement. He outlines a template from which we could all take pattern in our own response to the call of the Master. He saw the splendour of God and reverently worshipped Him. Acknowledging his insufficiencies, he readily repented and availed himself as God's messenger to Israel. Through his submission to the call, he agreed with God's plan for his life, wholeheartedly embracing true servanthood.

As you examine your life today, put priority on identifying the things that obscure your vision of God's true purpose for your life, the things that are not as obvious or easily discernible. Look deeper into the posture of your heart before God, and honestly evaluate whether it is bowed in submission and humility or steeped in pride and arrogance. Determinedly search out the Uzziahs that preoccupy your time and space and though well-intended, dethrone them from your life to give God pre-eminence. Desire to become a witness of His glory and His tabernacle of praise as you worship Him. It is what He requires of us all as His faithful servants.

> Therefore, since we are surrounded by so great a cloud
> of witnesses [who by faith have testified to the truth of
> God's absolute faithfulness], stripping off every
> unnecessary weight and the sin which so easily and
> cleverly entangles us, let us run with endurance and
> active persistence the race that is set before us,
> **Hebrews 12:1 (Amplified Bible)**

Day 36

Day 6
Called Before Conception

Jeremiah 1:5, 8–9, 17–19 (New King James Version)
[5]"Before I formed you in the womb I knew you;
Before you were born I sanctified you;
I ordained you a prophet to the nations."

[8]Do not be afraid of them, for I am with you and will rescue you," declares the Lord. [9]Then the Lord reached out his hand and touched my mouth and said to me, "I have put my words in your mouth.

[17]"Get yourself ready! Stand up and say to them whatever I command you. Do not be terrified by them, or I will terrify you before them. [18]Today I have made you a fortified city, an iron pillar and a bronze wall to stand against the whole land – against the kings of Judah, its officials, its priests and the people of the land. [19]They will fight against you but will not overcome you, for I am with you and will rescue you," declares the Lord.

I AM CERTAIN THAT WE can recollect that momentous day when we encountered our Lord and Saviour, Jesus Christ. Maybe some of us can recall every single detail of that life-changing and life-giving event as though it was yesterday. But even as we reminisce about the most memorable day of our lives, there is one aspect that we must acknowledge with the greatest humility and gratitude.

The day we met the Master was not the starting point of His relationship with us, and maybe it wasn't even our first interaction with Him. His eyes were always upon us, and He loved each of us long before we answered the call to fellowship with Him (1 John 4:19). He called us out of sin and away from a continuous degenerative existence to become His children even before being conceived in our mother's womb. Though it may have taken some of us longer than others to find our way to a reconciled life with Christ, in the realm that He exists where He foreknew us, He already declared who we would be and what we would become (Romans 8:29–30).

The Lord spoke these words plainly to Jeremiah; that He called and dedicated him as a prophet before his birth. God had already set him aside for a distinctive purpose; to proclaim His word at an appointed time to all people. Even today his words continue to minister to believers everywhere and the witness of the call of God before our conception is perpetuated. However, Jeremiah's initial response echoed his present weaknesses, inabilities, and shortcomings as he was unable to see himself the way that God saw him. Sometimes, even with the knowledge of this truth, we still have difficulty seeing ourselves the way that God already sees us. We get hung up, like Jeremiah, on the struggles and failures of our flesh that hinders our vision.

> **66Sometimes, even with the knowledge of this truth, we still have difficulty seeing ourselves the way that God already sees us.99**

How could one so young, clearly lacking the *gift of gab* be called to stand boldly before all of Israel; the young, the old, nobility and priesthood and proclaim *"THUS SAITH THE LORD!"* Jeremiah couldn't help but point out to the Lord that he was the wrong choice and clearly incapable of fulfilling His will if he answered this call. As Jeremiah informed the Lord of his error, the Lord exposed the stronghold that dictated his response, fear. The Lord then declared that there was no need for him to be afraid because the One who called him was already with him. As the Lord put forth His own hand and touched him, Jeremiah realized that he was the one holding up the train. All he had to do was avail himself to the call as the Lord foreordained. Furthermore, at that moment, the Lord gave him a hands-on training session, which he passed!

If we decisively pick apart our inherent desire within to convince God that He made a mistake in calling us, we too might find a spirit of fear at its root. The fear of being a failure, judged, rejected, alienated, ignored which I totally agree would have merit if we are expected to depend on human effort to accomplish God's purpose. In this regard, He placed an overcoming spirit of power, love, and a sound mind and personal discipline in us just as He did with Timothy (2 Timothy 1:7 Amplified Bible). Therefore, every obstacle we defy, every hurdle we cross, every time we come out victorious over our enemy, we endorse the truth of this scripture in our lives and triumph over the spirit of fear that comes to derail and destroy our purpose.

Paul also reminds us that we do not have to rely on our own strength. God is effectively working in us, equipping and enabling us to fulfil His divine purpose through the indwelling Spirit of Christ that needs no outside help (Philippians 2:13). Even when things don't seem at all realistic, our inept analysis of God's endless abilities always comes up short, as Jeremiah and others found out God doesn't need our help. All He needs is our faith in His ability to do, and with that mustard seed, He will prove to each of us that absolutely anything is possible if we only believe (Matthew 17:20).

For it is [not your strength, but it is] God who is effectively
at work in you, both to will and to work [that is, strengthening,
energizing, and creating in you the longing and the ability
to fulfill your purpose] for His good pleasure.
Philippians 2:13 (Amplified Bible)

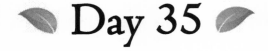 # Day 35

Day 7
Speak Lord, I'm Listening

1 Samuel 3:4–10 (New International Version)

[4]Then the Lord called Samuel. Samuel answered, "Here I am." [5]And he ran to Eli and said, "Here I am; you called me." But Eli said, "I did not call; go back and lie down." So he went and lay down.

[6]Again the Lord called, "Samuel!" And Samuel got up and went to Eli and said, "Here I am; you called me."

"My son," Eli said, "I did not call; go back and lie down."

[7]Now Samuel did not yet know the Lord: The word of the Lord had not yet been revealed to him.

[8]A third time the Lord called, "Samuel!" And Samuel got up and went to Eli and said, "Here I am; you called me." Then Eli realized that the Lord was calling the boy.

[9]So Eli told Samuel, "Go and lie down, and if he calls you, say, 'Speak, Lord, for your servant is listening.'" So Samuel went and lay down in his place.

[10]The Lord came and stood there, calling as at the other times, "Samuel! Samuel!" Then Samuel said, "Speak, for your servant is listening."

*S*AMUEL'S BIRTH WAS no ordinary occurrence. His mother, Hannah, had the complete devotion of a husband who loved her immeasurably, but she suffered many years of disappointment, pain, and anguish because it seemed that the one thing she desperately wanted she could not have. However, her dire circumstances were filled with opportunity, giving rise to the faith that she needed to believe God for an extraordinary child. This son she would dedicate even before his conception to service in the house of God all the days of his life as a token of faith (1 Samuel 1:11) which she declared and celebrated in her song of thanksgiving(1 Samuel 2:1–10).

The timing of Samuel's birth was no coincidence although to Hannah, it seemed long in coming. Undeniably, at that time there was a more than noticeable drought for the spoken word of the Lord to Israel because of the sinful lives of Eli's sons. This void that was created had to be filled and the Lord needed a choice vessel through whom he could once again speak to His people. Unaware of his calling to be a prophet, Samuel spent his days obediently learning from Eli who years earlier gave hope to his childless, broken-hearted mother. But while he spoke to her as the oracle of God confirming the blessing to come from her womb, he did nothing to eradicate the wanton and abhorrent sin of his sons Hophni and Phinehas, themselves priests, in the house of God.

> **66God can call us to do anything at any time during any stage of our lives as we are never too old or too young to hear His voice or do His will.99**

God can call us to do anything at any time during any stage of our lives as we are never too old or too young to hear His voice or do His will. It was through Samuel the Lord was able to break His silence, speaking once again to the future of Israel and ending Eli's lineage. Youth and naiveté aside, God was ready to use Samuel, the one whom He sent as a blessing to a barren woman. He is interested in available vessels, willing to be used to fulfil His purpose in the earth, and He does not need to meet any publicly acceptable criterion, age or otherwise. He has the authority to remove and establish people as He sees fit regardless of the Christian example(s) before us or the void created by the lack of it, and rank is clearly a non-issue. He withdraws privilege by linage when it is mistaken for entitlement and appoints whomever He chooses. Hence, we remain with only one personal challenge, acceptance by our obedience.

There are many excuses we could use with supposed legitimacy to validate our unavailability and inability. But in their most basic form, they are just excuses; self-imposed justifications and limitations that hinder God from using and blessing us. So herein lies the challenge when we recognize that God is calling us to purpose; do we humbly submit to His voice in the still of the night when He calls us, ready to hear His instruction? Or, do we cower and retreat into the comfort of our present administrations in the house of the Lord indicating that we are already doing enough for God and He should find another vessel?

Well, my friend, the truth is, God is unimpressed by our ability to execute devout rituals that cannot produce the repentant lifestyle that draws us closer to Him. He takes no pleasure in any service from us that lacks godly reverence and worship with its meaning lost in tradition (Isaiah 29:13; Matthew 15:8). But, He can certainly move in our midst and through us when we choose to become a man or woman ready and willing to say, *"Speak Lord, I'm listening"*. Tune into the voice of the Lord and believe me, you will know it when you hear it by the Holy

Spirit's discernment (John 10:27). He will guide us in the paths of truth as we walk in obedience to Him, and we will never be ashamed. Just as the Lord called Samuel to be Israel's prophet then, He will confirm our call to His service now before all men. Just one question, *"Are you listening?"*

> But I will raise up for Myself a faithful priest who will
> do according to what is in My heart and in My soul;
> and I will build him a permanent and enduring house,
> and he will walk before My anointed forever.
> **1 Samuel 2:53 (Amplified Bible)**

Day 34

Day 8
The Disgraced Deliverer

Exodus 3:1–14 (New King James Version)

⁷And the Lord said: "I have surely seen the oppression of My people who are in Egypt, and have heard their cry because of their taskmasters, for I know their sorrows. ⁸So I have come down to deliver them out of the hand of the Egyptians, and to bring them up from that land to a good and large land, to a land flowing with milk and honey, to the place of the Canaanites and the Hittites and the Amorites and the Perizzites and the Hivites and the Jebusites. ⁹Now therefore, behold, the cry of the children of Israel has come to Me, and I have also seen the oppression with which the Egyptians oppress them. ¹⁰Come now, therefore, and I will send you to Pharaoh that you may bring My people, the children of Israel, out of Egypt." ¹¹But Moses said to God, "Who am I that I should go to Pharaoh, and that I should bring the children of Israel out of Egypt?"

¹²So He said, "I will certainly be with you. And this shall be a sign to you that I have sent you: When you have brought the people out of Egypt, you shall serve God on this mountain."

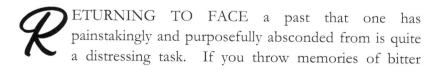

RETURNING TO FACE a past that one has painstakingly and purposefully absconded from is quite a distressing task. If you throw memories of bitter experiences and the possibility of life-threatening consequences in the mix, well now you have real problems! Even more exasperating is the voice of God instructing you to return to that place you fled decades earlier, informing you that He has called you to be the deliverer of those whom you left behind. Fully aware that they would remember why you bolted in the first place, you begin to relive the repressed flashbacks of your last moments there, and you become inundated by fear. If he had a choice, certainly Moses would have retorted, *"No way, José!"* and bolted yet again. Actually, he wasted no time to tell God please, send someone else, anybody else but me! (Exodus 4:13)

I am sure that anyone in Moses' place would have given God the same response, irrespective of the phenomenal burning bush that triggered their conversation. *"How could I go back there? Wouldn't they remember what I did? What qualifies me for leadership? Who would listen to a fugitive and a failure?"* Agreeably, these are all very plausible and legitimate questions that anyone can find understandable under his highly peculiar circumstances. He invested forty long years into building a new life away from the tragic events of a past that he made every effort to forget. Even with the damaging evidence mounted against him in Egypt, God handpicked this murderer and fugitive, turned shepherd, to become the deliverer that His children were crying out for.

We all have a skeleton (or twenty) in our past that we are not too proud off or are downright ashamed to even think about, but their existence does not alter what God sees when He looks at us. Sometimes our obedience to His call reroutes us to specific areas in our past that we would rather forget or circumvent. But it's right in those condemned places that we would find people who have been ceaselessly asking and waiting for a deliverance that is greater than our disgrace. What we would also realize is that regardless of where our obedience takes us, through the complete and restorative work of Christ we are free from our entanglement with the guilt and shame that we once experienced there.

It's astonishing how a distant memory combined with guilt and shame can inject us with immediate psychological paralysis. Together, they can recreate a slow and agonizing journey through the mineshaft of our weaknesses, flaws, and faults; aggressively working to subdue the conqueror within that God has already empowered us to become. Although Moses meticulously listed all the valid reasons why he was the wrong choice for this assignment, God responded with His everlasting promise declared to all generations, "...I am the Lord [you have the promise of My changeless omnipotence and faithfulness]." (Exodus 6:8 Amplified Bible)

> **66When we step out in faith and obedience God's unlimited power and faithfulness become our vanguard; whatever we encounter, He is right there with us.99**

When we step out in faith and obedience God's unlimited power and faithfulness become our vanguard, whatever we encounter, He is right there with us. He confirmed this truth when He told Moses His name that day, "I AM WHO I AM" and "I WILL BE WHAT I WILL BE" (Exodus 3:14 Amplified Bible, Classic Edition) the eternally present and future tense God who is and will forever be with us. In essence, He leaves nothing in our lives to chance by establishing that He always fulfils what He has ordained.

Do not be distressed by the call and try to measure your suitability by your past, or seek to satisfy man's requirements for fulfilling your God-ordained mission. We will never meet the standards. Instead, focus on the privilege of being called and that He singled you out to make His name great through your obedience. God is the one who calls and therefore, the only one who can equip us for the call. We certainly cannot do it for ourselves. Believe me, when we see what God can achieve through a humble imperfect vessel, we'll be totally awestruck by the miracle He's turned each of us into! All we are required to do is submit He'll do the rest; He's the only one who can.

[5]I am the Lord, and there is no one else; there is no God besides Me. I will gird and arm you, though you have not known Me, [6]That men may know from the east and the rising of the sun and from the west and the setting of the sun that there is no God besides Me. I am the Lord, and no one else [is He].
Isaiah 45:5–6 (Amplified Bible)

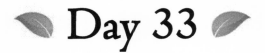

Day 33

Day 9
Divine Appointment

1 Samuel 16:1, 4–7 (New King James Version)

¹Now the LORD said to Samuel, "How long will you mourn for Saul, seeing I have rejected him from reigning over Israel? Fill your horn with oil, and go; I am sending you to Jesse the Bethlehemite. For I have provided Myself a king among his sons."

⁴So Samuel did what the LORD said, and went to Bethlehem. And the elders of the town trembled at his coming, and said, "Do you come peaceably?"
⁵And he said, "Peaceably; I have come to sacrifice to the LORD. Sanctify yourselves, and come with me to the sacrifice." Then he consecrated Jesse and his sons, and invited them to the sacrifice.
⁶So it was, when they came, that he looked at Eliab and said, "Surely the LORD's anointed is before Him!"
⁷But the LORD said to Samuel, "Do not look at his appearance or at his physical stature, because I have refused him. For the Lord does not see as man sees; for man looks at the outward appearance, but the LORD looks at the heart."

AVID WAS THE one that nobody saw. He was considered the least of his household and given the task of livestock duty. As an afterthought, forgotten in the wilderness amidst the sheep, his life was almost void of any real human companionship. In the desert, he could be conveniently ignored and overlooked by his father and brothers. As such, his presence at the sacrifice with the Prophet was completely unnecessary. An even greater preposterous thought would be for him to stand in the line-up before Samuel for consideration as King Saul's successor.

David was, without a doubt, the least likely candidate amongst all the possibilities of Jesse's lineage to be anointed as king. After all, any one of his seven robust polished older brothers would be a more appropriate contender for this monumental ascent to the throne with ease. Nobody anticipated in their wildest imagination that the one most disfavoured and disregarded by man would be the one highly favoured by God; His prime choice, His friend.

Maybe you have been there; a life-changing opportunity emerged, and both your peers and superiors ignore your eligibility when God already selected you. But through His grace and favour in one strategic move, God creates a path that miraculously deposits you in plain view and ahead of those who purposefully snubbed you. As the questioning eyebrows greet your arrival, God reiterates the admonishment He gave to Samuel as he stood before Jesse's finest. It is easy to impress mortals with a sophisticated exterior and cultured behaviour, but it is the posture of our hearts before God, our comeliness within that qualifies us for His use.

We may feel that our usefulness to God is elusive and limited at best, especially with our recurrent personal let-downs. Like

David, we sometimes contend with issues of loneliness, envy, and bullying simply because those around us do not understand God's ways and His plans. We may even think that they have the power to dictate our progress when their behaviour is really a part of God's character development plan for us. These days of preparation may seem both tedious and rigorous and more so when our God-ordained purpose is not as clearly defined as we had hoped. But in spite of these challenges, we must choose to trust Him totally, the one who has strategically positioned us to develop the spiritual maturity and wisdom needed for what lies ahead, proving that indeed all things work together for our good (Romans 8:28).

> **"It is easy to impress mortals... but it is the posture of our hearts before God, our comeliness within that qualifies us for His use."**

That day at the sacrifice, Samuel revealed David's call to the throne in the midst of his flabbergasted family members. However, his journey to becoming Israel's monarch began while he was a recluse, dutifully leading sheep in solitude where he was transformed into man after God's own heart (1 Samuel 13:14; Acts 13:22). Through all his difficult experiences, scouting the arid plains for adequate grassland and warding off vicious predators, David learned to find refuge and solace in his God. He developed a personal relationship with God through his worshipful spirit and honoured Him with a life of humility.

Through a shepherd's calling, David allowed God to mould him into the leader that would successfully and justly lead Israel in time to come. As he availed himself for God's Spirit to guide

him, we are encouraged to do likewise even if we do not see His
entire plan or its end. God is faithful to bring us through our
greatest challenges if we allow Him to. David submitted to God
and he was openly exalted while astounded onlookers stood by.
No one present, not even Samuel knew the way this encounter
would have turned out. We may think we are the least favoured,
but God sees our potential and worth when men brush us aside.
I am convinced that He knows exactly what He is doing, *"… so
Lord, let it be done according to Your will."*

⁴David was thirty years old when he became king,
and he reigned forty years. ⁵In Hebron he reigned
over Judah seven years and six months, and in Jerusalem
he reigned thirty-three years over all Israel and Judah.
2 Samuel 5:4–5 (Amplified Bible)

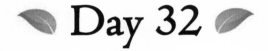 # Day 32

Day 10
Exponential Potential

John 6:5, 8–13 (Amplified Bible)

⁵Jesus looked up and saw that a large crowd was coming toward Him, and He said to Philip, "Where will we buy bread for these people to eat?"

⁸One of His disciples, Andrew, Simon Peter's brother, said to Him, ⁹"There is a little boy here who has five barley loaves and two fish; but what are these for so many people?" ¹⁰Jesus said, "Have the people sit down [to eat]." Now [the ground] there was [covered with] an abundance of grass, so the men sat down, about 5,000 in number. ¹¹Then Jesus took the loaves, and when He had given thanks, He distributed them to those who were seated; the same also with the fish, as much as they wanted. ¹²When they had eaten enough, He said to His disciples, "Gather up the leftover pieces so that nothing will be lost." ¹³So they gathered them up, and they filled twelve large baskets with pieces from the five barley loaves which were left over by those who had eaten.

*W*E DO NOT KNOW much about the little boy in this miraculous event, not even his name. However, the scripture tells us that he left home with a meal-for-one packed and ended up in the colossal multitude following Jesus.

He probably made plans for his day, maybe to catch fish or explore the hillside with his friends. But, by God's strategic alignment, he was amongst the crowd in those moments unaware that his pint-sized two-course meal would be serving him as well as the population of a small country. When Jesus' disciple, Andrew unearthed his meagre provisions, despite its ineffable inadequacy and with nothing else to offer, it was this finding he presented to the Master to feed the vast assembly that stood before them.

Improbable? Surely.
Unfathomable? Certainly.
Impossible? With God, never!

We don't always like being singled out from the crowd, especially when we think our resources or the skills required for meeting widely publicized needs come up short. Words like incapable, unsuitable and unqualified get flung around so quickly and easily by those lining the periphery of the same situation, waiting like vultures to pick apart our failure. Such declarations can saturate us with doubt in an instant, especially if we use the evident realities to validate our contribution, and sometimes with good reason. But when we allow doubt to prevail and hitch all our chances of success, or even survival to the wagon of our human abilities, we upstage the limitless power of our God.

This situation clearly teaches us that we will never see our offerings, gifts and talents expand to their fullest potential unless we totally release them (and ourselves) into the hands of the Master. Holding on to our bread and fish would certainly meet our needs for the moment, quelling our fears of inadequacy and fulfilling short-term self-preservation. However, when we submit, we give God the most excellent opportunity to apply His exponential power to our lowliest of offerings. In that instant what we may consider being a pathetic move on our part can, by faith, produce supernatural growth and expansion above and beyond our finite capacity and expectations.

> **66...we will never see our offerings, gifts and talents expand to their fullest potential unless we totally release them (and ourselves) into the hands of the Master.99**

When it comes to giving, it is impossible for us to out-give God. Everything good and perfect that we have received, whether we choose to believe it or not, came from the Father above (James 1:17) because He is an expert at giving the best. There is no gift greater than the redemption Christ made available to all by dying for our sins on Calvary. His sacrifice represents the epitome of God's boundless love for man. In humility, this little boy also gave all that he had to the Master, and a miracle took place right in their midst when his simple meal came into contact with Jesus.

Who can foreknow what God will do when we say yes to Him as an act of faith by giving him what we hold in our hands? Is it possible that we are pivoting between yes and no because of fear of the unknown and holding back on releasing what God has given to us? There is no need for fear when we understand that submission to God is all about love and increase, not domination and loss. As we respond in humility, we showcase God's greatness and bring glory to His name. The bystanders that look on curiously to see the outcome will witness and even be blessed by the true power of our God at work in us. All He needs is a willing vessel.

Let's focus on pleasing the Master today by simply saying, "*I surrender, Lord. I'm your servant and all that I have is Yours to be used for Your honour and glory.*" You will be glad that you did, and He will be satisfied with your offering.

Teach me to do Your will [so that I may
please You], For You are my God;
Let Your good Spirit lead me on level ground.
Psalm 143:10 (Amplified Bible)

 # Day 31

Day 11
Salvation Invasion

1 Kings 17:9–16 (Amplified Bible)

[9]"Arise, go to Zarephath, which belongs to Sidon, and stay there. Behold, I have commanded a widow there to provide for you." [10]So he set out and went to Zarephath, and when he came to the gate of the city, behold, a widow was there gathering sticks [for firewood]. He called out to her and said, "Please bring me a little water in a jar, so that I may drink." [11]As she was going to get it, he called to her and said, "Please bring me a piece of bread in your hand." [12]But she said, "As the Lord your God lives, I have no bread, only a handful of flour in the bowl and a little oil in the jar. See, I am gathering a few sticks so that I may go in and bake it for me and my son, that we may eat it [as our last meal] and die."

[13]Elijah said to her, "Do not fear; go and do as you have said. Just make me a little bread from it first and bring it out to me, and afterward you may make one for yourself and for your son. [14]For this is what the Lord God of Israel says: 'The bowl of flour shall not be exhausted nor shall the jar of oil be empty until the day that the Lord sends rain [again] on the face of the earth.'" [15]She went and did as Elijah said. And she and he and her household ate for many days. [16]The bowl of flour was not exhausted nor did the jar of oil become empty, in accordance with the word of the Lord which He spoke through Elijah.

*W*ITH HER THOUGHTS to herself, she knew that this was the very last time she would gather her firewood. In her mind ideas of imminent death swirled around, an unavoidable eventuality of the intense drought throughout the region. Her downcast eyes had already measured the scanty remnants of food in the pantry that was just enough for two (her and her son) and after this final meal, they had no hope for survival. She left her home and began her ultimate journey towards the city gates. At the same time, the Prophet instructed by the Lord left the Brook Cherith and also began his journey towards the city gates, to find her. Whereas she thought she was making her last trek to gather sticks, she was really en route to a divine encounter that would assuredly change the course of her life, extending it in the process.

She is not alone in her resolve. Facing the veracity of an impossible situation happens across our paths every now and then. We look at the conditions that confront us: a financial crisis, a final deadline, a crumbling marriage, a rebellious child, a devastating error, and wonder about their outcomes. These are the terminal sentences preceding the irreversible *'game-over'* informing us the end is not near, it's here. But even as we stand by helplessly watching the gears make their penultimate turn before screeching to a grinding halt, the supernatural deliverance only possible through the power and presence of the Almighty God arrives on the scene. Albeit, sometimes the deliverance we so desperately need come in packages that we may not quite expect or comprehend.

Elijah arrived at the gate of the city of Zarephath. Maybe she saw him, maybe she didn't, but she would definitely heed his voice. He purposefully walked towards her and invaded her morose thoughts with a request that sounded extremely advantageous and self-gratifying, and of a widow of all persons! The gossipers of the day would have torn his good name to shreds as they questioned each other in the marketplace; "*What kind of Prophet is he to demand food from the widow and fatherless to fatten himself up in these, the leanest of times? What God could he be serving with that selfish attitude?*"

But the slander wouldn't have mattered to him as he was the kind of Prophet that obeyed God despite the consequences. In fact, it was at his command the drought began and came to an end when God wanted to deal with King Ahab's idolatry (1 Kings 17:1, 18:1, 41). This exchange between Elijah and the widow created a divine opportunity for God to intervene in her grim situation and deliver this lowly

> **66When we do not understand God's methodology we may unknowingly wreck our deliverance.99**

family from the jaws of death. Although she protested at first, through her eventual compliance, she too released God's hand to perform the miracle she so desperately needed. What a profound example of the love of God!

When we do not understand God's methodology we may unknowingly wreck our deliverance. We must remember that His thoughts and His ways are not limited to our finite human imaginations and accept at times that we are incapable of tracing His hand and anticipating His plan. Despite the Prophet's most unorthodox proposition, we recognize that we do not necessarily trust in the method per se. We are blessed when we believe God and honour the word of His true servants (2 Chronicles 20:20). Once we trust Him with everything, He will never disappoint us with anything.

The least of our concerns is the means through which our breakthroughs come. If we could know and see all things, then where would our faith in God and submission to His sovereignty rank? What is most important, however, is for us to be confident in the fact that He cares for us much more than we could comprehend. Let's allow Him to do what He does best, take care of those who are His own. It is the most magnificent display of love we will ever encounter.

[19]And my God will liberally supply (fill until full) your
every need according to His riches in glory in Christ Jesus.
[20]To our God and Father be the glory forever and ever.
Amen.
Philippians 4:19–20 (Amplified Bible)

Day 30

Day 12
Positional Advantage

Luke 19:1–10 (New King James Version)

¹Then Jesus entered and passed through Jericho. ²Now behold, there was a man named Zacchaeus who was a chief tax collector, and he was rich. ³And he sought to see who Jesus was, but could not because of the crowd, for he was of short stature. ⁴So he ran ahead and climbed up into a sycamore tree to see Him, for He was going to pass that way. ⁵And when Jesus came to the place, He looked up and saw him, and said to him, "Zacchaeus, make haste and come down, for today I must stay at your house." ⁶So he made haste and came down, and received Him joyfully. ⁷But when they saw it, they all complained, saying, "He has gone to be a guest with a man who is a sinner."

⁸Then Zacchaeus stood and said to the Lord, "Look, Lord, I give half of my goods to the poor; and if I have taken anything from anyone by false accusation, I restore fourfold."

⁹And Jesus said to him, "Today salvation has come to this house, because he also is a son of Abraham; ¹⁰for the Son of Man has come to seek and to save that which was lost."

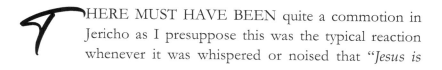

THERE MUST HAVE BEEN quite a commotion in Jericho as I presuppose this was the typical reaction whenever it was whispered or noised that "*Jesus is*

here! The Master is here!" I am equally certain it was an arduous task for anyone to get close or even stay close to Him because of the multitudes that reportedly thronged Him. So first, imagine being in that clamouring mob following Jesus. Now, imagine being noticeably short under normal circumstances and consider your options. Even someone of average height can be effortlessly overpowered by such a potentially uncontrollable crowd in a stampede, pushed and pulled all over in unintended directions. Yet amid these circumstances, a vertically-challenged Zacchaeus with a slim-to-no-chance wanted to see who this Jesus was.

One could never tell, maybe this would be his only opportunity. Who could guarantee that the Master would ever return to this region? And this was one occasion when his social status provided no assurances. Neither his position nor his financial standing could guarantee him any favour or a '*shoo-in*' for a front-row seat to see Jesus. He had to '*wing it*' like everybody else and that was no easy task, or was it?

When we experience impossible situations we are pressed to search for alternatives if we truly desire to attain our goals. As Zacchaeus reasoned out the matter, he decided his best or only option was to change his position. In so doing, he accessed a clear line of vision to the Master that simultaneously gave the Master a clear view of him. While Zacchaeus was preoccupied with being able to see Jesus he soon realized that more importantly, Jesus wanted to see him; not just fulfil a heartfelt wish, but to introduce him to the grace that the Master came to grant every sinner. Based on the response by the religious faction, it was clear that the real purpose of their meeting was unpopular. They could not understand why one so pure and holy with so much to offer would want to be, of all places, at the home of such a vile and publicly hated sinner.

We may feel that we are no match for the obstacles we are up against; too small, too weak, too helpless or even too sinful to make an ounce of difference. Zacchaeus by his actions was the first to acknowledge his limitations, but the fact that he was not willing to accept defeat shows us that we can overcome negative situations even when there are variables that we cannot change. But through unconventional methods he was able to change his position and increase his visibility, thereby achieving his goal. Though the throng contained many hopefuls, the one who altered his position was the one Jesus saw and whom He also welcomed into the blessed joy of fellowship with Him.

Whenever we encounter obstructions that could impede our view of the Lord, we can apply this model that Zacchaeus demonstrated. His eyes are upon on us (Psalm 32:8, 1 Peter 3:12), and He sees what we go through day by day, so let us deliberately and strategically position ourselves in the Master's line of vision to receive direction from Him. Let us commit to being fervent in prayer, supplications, fasting and obedience. As we wait for Him to meet the deep-seated needs in our hearts, He is also waiting for us to change from our comfortable, predictable daily routines into a deeper and more meaningful relationship with Him.

> **66...the one who altered his position was the one Jesus saw and whom He also welcomed into the blessed joy of fellowship with Him.99**

The opportunity to change is right before us, within our grasp. Now is the time for the Master to come in, commune with and minister to us. We can't get to Him through the crowd, but in our single-minded persistence to humbly submit our weaknesses to Him we will attract His grace (2 Corinthians 12:9–11). His ear is ever so attuned to hear the silent cry of a worshipful heart. Jesus is passing your way today, be prepared to receive Him and fellowship in His love and grace.

But to as many as did receive and welcome Him,
He gave the authority (power, privilege, right) to become
the children of God, that is, to those who believe in
(adhere to, trust in, and rely on) His name—
John 1:12 (Amplified Bible, Classic Edition)

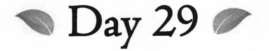

Day 29

Day 13
Come Forth

John 11:32, 39–44 (New King James Version)

[32]Then, when Mary came where Jesus was, and saw Him, she fell down at His feet, saying to Him, "Lord, if You had been here, my brother would not have died."

[39]Jesus said, "Take away the stone." Martha, the sister of him who was dead, said to Him, "Lord, by this time there is a stench, for he has been dead four days." [40]Jesus said to her, "Did I not say to you that if you would believe you would see the glory of God?" [41]Then they took away the stone from the place where the dead man was lying. And Jesus lifted up His eyes and said, "Father, I thank You that You have heard Me. [42]And I know that You always hear Me, but because of the people who are standing by I said this, that they may believe that You sent Me." [43]Now when He had said these things, He cried with a loud voice, "Lazarus, come forth!" [44]And he who had died came out bound hand and foot with grave clothes, and his face was wrapped with a cloth. Jesus said to them, "Loose him, and let him go."

WE TRULY RECOGNISE the limitations of our humanness when we are face to face with a mess that needs supernatural intervention. We can often overlook petitioning God's involvement in the simple issues of the day that we can reason out and remedy by ourselves. After all, these inconsequential matters are well within our scope for resolution and we therefore often neglect to consult God for guidance. But when the challenge goes well beyond all our capabilities and we are unable to find a solution, we can feel dreadfully helpless to the point where we think it is impossible, even for God, to turn it around in our favour.

Broken-hearted and grief-stricken Mary fell at the feet of the Master. It was all over as the outcome had already taken effect, and the worst-case scenario was their conclusion. Lazarus' sickness was too severe, succumbing to its final blow of death. They sent word to Jesus about his condition and waited anxiously for His arrival. Through their close relationship, they knew Him to be the Healer so the family was certain He could handle this situation. But in the end, and without forming the words with their mouths, they placed a limit on His power in their hearts. Now that days had passed, how could He bring back a corpse that was already in a state of decomposition? This time no consultation was necessary; of course, it was impossible!

We may also have areas in our lives where we have also accepted their current state to be our final verdict. Maybe the situation has been diagnosed as terminal with no way out, or it has already been pronounced dead and too much time has passed to resuscitate whatever remains. Then consequently, we have no other option but to accept the foreseeable outcome because absolutely nothing further can be done. We don't have to be a rocket scientist or Nobel laureate to know that, it's just plain old common sense.

However, we are reminded today that where there is no way, there is only one way made available to us through our awesome God who is unrestricted by time and unlimited in power. He is the only one capable of accomplishing the impossible with the ability to return life to any deadness, wherever it may occur. Whether it is a lost once-in-a-lifetime opportunity, an unending season of sickness or waiting for an answer that would come too late; God can give us another chance to receive and embrace what we thought was gone forever.

> **66...where there is no way, there is only one way available to us through our awesome God who is unrestricted by time and unlimited in power.99**

As the Master instructs it to *"Come forth!"* in our lives, absolutely nothing can stop it, we just need to unwrap it when it arrives.

When Jesus restored life to the four-day-old corpse of Lazarus, He presented a new perspective on the power of God to the onlookers and furthermore, His love and compassion for humanity. They had an opportunity to see the true glory and nature of God manifest right before their eyes and witnessed the value He placed on relationships and family ties. This same restorative life-giving power is available to every one of us who call on and believe in the name of Jesus Christ, placing faith in God the Father through Him. Paul confirms this when he admonished the Roman church that if the Spirit of the one who raised Christ from death lives in us, we will in turn have this same life in our mortal bodies (Romans 8:10–11).

So, as we believe God today to obtain our miracles at His hands, let us be obedient to His voice and roll away all the elements of fear, doubt and unbelief that block His entry into our dark places. Just stand back and allow God to gain all the glory and honour for what He has already released into our lives and we are about to receive by faith.

Jesus said to him, "[You say to Me,] 'If You can?' All things are possible for the one who believes and trusts [in Me]!"
Mark 9:23 (Amplified Bible)

Day 28

Day 14
Kindness Begets Blessings

2 Kings 4:11–17 (Amplified Bible)

[11]One day he came there and turned in to the upper room and lay down to rest. [12]And he said to Gehazi his servant, "Call this Shunammite." So he called her and she stood before him. [13]Now he said to Gehazi, "Say to her now, 'You have gone to all this trouble for us; what can I do for you? Would you like to be mentioned to the king or to the captain of the army? " She answered, "I live among my own people [in peace and security and need no special favors]."

[14]Later Elisha said, "What then is to be done for her?" Gehazi answered, "Well, she has no son and her husband is old." [15]He said, "Call her." So Gehazi called her, and she [came and] stood in the doorway.

[16]Elisha said, "At this season next year, you will embrace a son." She said, "No, my lord. O man of God, do not lie to your maidservant."

[17]But the woman conceived and gave birth to a son at that season the next year, just as Elisha had said to her.

THE SHUNAMMITE was a distinguished and affluential woman that enjoyed a more than comfortable lifestyle in her homeland. She contentedly extended kindness to a stranger without expecting any repayment for her generosity having recognised that he was no ordinary man but a holy man of the God of Israel. She went as far as requesting her husband to renovate their home to provide better accommodations; greater comfort and increased privacy for Prophet Elisha and Gehazi, his servant. Still, she never asked him for anything in return for the various adjustments they willingly made to their lives. Her care and concern toward the Prophet were of her own volition. While she may have believed her actions represented simple thoughtfulness, they provided an avenue for her kindness to be rewarded in an extraordinary manner. She was about to receive a blessing that would fulfil a desire deep in the recesses of her heart and change her life forever.

Kindness is a character trait identified in the fruit of the Holy Spirit (Galatians 5:22–23), and we cannot always anticipate its effect on the persons who receive it at our hands or their response. Our Lord Jesus Christ teaches us how to be kind and show compassion to the people around us through His example (Matthew 9:36) and the Holy Spirit's indwelling (John 14:26). Moreover, like the Shunammite, once we sow kindness we will also reap kindness, manifesting in unexpectant blessings that we probably gave up on ever receiving.

Prophet Elisha sent for her to express his gratitude, and her response was unchanged as she relayed her contentment to him. But he did not let it go and their careful observation revealed a void in her life that she had accepted and come to terms with it in her own way. So much so, in her immediate response to Elisha's declaration that this void would be filled she relived the pain that preceded her present resolve. She was deeply affected by his words that declared she would have a son and begged him not to give her false hope, for she had already given up hope. Despite her initial protests rooted in the pain of her past, she finally experienced the joy of his words changing her future when the appointed time came for her to receive her promised blessing.

By showing kindness to others when we observe a need, regardless of how simple it may seem in our eyes, we must be ever so mindful that through our actions we are establishing God's glory in the earth. When we selflessly avail ourselves to His Spirit, He can use us as His voice and hands to minister and touch the lives of others that open doors for even greater blessings in our own lives. Nothing we do for God or investment we make in His kingdom goes unnoticed or unrewarded (Matthew 10: 40–42).

We have already received God's favour through salvation by the grace of our Lord Jesus Christ. As we become more like Him through the indwelling witness of the Holy Spirit, the resultant kindness we show will bless others and generate more kindness. But by the Shunammite's example, we must not limit our harvest by only looking to the places we've sown to be blessed by the fruit that it yields. This practice could usher in the conditionality associated with works, nullifying the effect of grace as we could easily attribute the blessings we receive to be a direct result of what we have done.

> **"By showing kindness to others when we observe a need ... we must be ever so mindful that through our actions we are establishing God's glory in the earth."**

Instead, let us always give as unto the Lord with our primary intent being that we must please Him and Him only. As you receive each blessing, thankfully acknowledge that God's hands have released it to you and that it pleases Him to ceaselessly provide His children with all things for us to enjoy (1 Timothy 6:17-18). So joyfully look to God exclusively as your source of blessings and receive them all with a heart of humility and gratitude.

So, as God's own chosen people, who are holy [set apart, sanctified for His purpose] and well-beloved [by God Himself], put on a heart of compassion, kindness, humility, gentleness, and patience [which has the power to endure whatever injustice or unpleasantness comes, with good temper];
Colossians 3:12 (Amplified Bible)

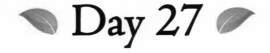

Day 27

Day 15
Blessed and Highly Favoured

Luke 1:28–38 (Amplified Bible)

[28]And coming to her, the angel said, "Greetings, favored one! The Lord is with you." [29]But she was greatly perplexed at what he said, and kept carefully considering what kind of greeting this was.

[30]The angel said to her, "Do not be afraid, Mary, for you have found favor with God. [31]Listen carefully: you will conceive in your womb and give birth to a son, and you shall name Him Jesus. [32]He will be great and eminent and will be called the Son of the Most High; and the Lord God will give Him the throne of His father David; [33]and He will reign over the house of Jacob (Israel) forever, and of His kingdom there shall be no end."

[34]Mary said to the angel, "How will this be, since I am a virgin and have no intimacy with any man?" [35]Then the angel replied to her, "The Holy Spirit will come upon you, and the power of the Most High will overshadow you [like a cloud]; for that reason the holy (pure, sinless) Child shall be called the Son of God. [36]And listen, even your relative Elizabeth has also conceived a son in her old age; and she who was called barren is now in her sixth month. [37]For with God nothing [is or ever] shall be impossible." [38]Then Mary said, "Behold, I am the servant of the Lord; may it be done to me according to your word." And the angel left her.

*W*HAT AN INCREDIBLE event! A young woman in one of the most exciting phases of her life must consider the possibility of losing everything, maybe even her very life, if she chooses to submit to God's plan for her. This assignment was unprecedented, unlike anything experienced throughout the entire history of humanity. Mary was in a situation that was light years beyond her comfort zone with no model to follow. As a Jewess, she would have grown up with the knowledge that one day Messiah (Christ, Anointed One) would come. The time and the means probably never crossed her mind, least of all that she would carry him in her very own womb.

The message that the angel delivered to Mary confounded her. However, she did not focus on the obvious puzzling questions like whether the messenger was indeed God-sent, whether the message was true or not or why she was hand-picked. Her foremost concern was how the content of the message would be fulfilled, which she readily questioned. She was fully aware that according to the laws of nature, the statements made to her were absolutely impossible! Nevertheless, the angel satisfied her with the answers she sought. Mary immediately submitted to the plan of God and accepted her assignment, notwithstanding the consequence that the law demanded, she and the child could die.

We've each been called to fulfil some aspect of God's will in the earth, and let's face it, sometimes we really don't like or appreciate the assignments that He hands out to us. They can appear weird or bizarre, lacking the loftiness we expect to be synonymous with our status, void of fanfare, and questionable on every level. *"How could God ask me to do that? Who would understand the call? Who would believe this is the will of God? Who would support me?"* The solitude of the journey ahead can easily overshadow purpose as the cheer of the crowd around us dissipates into nothingness and the whistle in the wind becomes the only audible sound in the room.

This aspect of the Master's call can definitely be touted as the most unfavourable as it can unquestionably make us feel like a rudderless ship, but it can simultaneously be the most rewarding. How so? It is in these circumstances that we develop an acute awareness of the Master's voice to receive His guidance and instructions. It actually becomes a lifeline as the only means by which we would be able to achieve what He has called us to do. We learn to draw closer to Him to hear the still small voice as He continually reveals His perfect plan and gives us strategies for the way forward. As we strip away the buffers of knowledge, status, ability and entitlement indeed we might find ourselves inept, charting the course through new and unfamiliar territory. But, in coming to the Father with childlike openness uncompromised by the shroud of self-actualization, our submission pleases Him. This behaviour becomes our token of true humility, exhibiting our understanding that His plans are higher than ours (Isaiah 55:8–9).

> **"We learn to draw closer to Him to hear the still small voice as He continually reveals His perfect plan and gives us strategies for the way forward."**

The call of God upon every individual would manifest in variant ways – to carry the Messiah like Mary, to preserve a lineage and lead a kingdom like Joseph, to impart truth like Paul, to succeed leadership like Joshua or to deliver a nation like Moses. Whatever the nature of your call, the most significant factor is your response. Mary's ultimate response affirmed her faith in God and not the impossibility of His request. Her character was tried and proven by the definitive declaration that concluded her discourse, confirming that she was indeed the favoured choice among all her peers to birth the Saviour of the world. Through her humility the gift of salvation would come to all humankind, exhibiting by her faith that absolutely nothing is impossible with God.

[46]And Mary said, "My soul magnifies and exalts the Lord,
[47]And my spirit has rejoiced in God my Savior.
[48] "For He has looked [with loving care] on the humble state of His maidservant; For behold, from now on all generations will count me blessed and happy and favored by God!
Luke 1:46–48 (Amplified Bible)

Day 26

Day 16
Context Clarity

John 4:7–14 (Amplified Bible)

[7]Then a woman from Samaria came to draw water. Jesus said to her, "Give Me a drink" [8]For His disciples had gone off into the city to buy food [9]The Samaritan woman asked Him, "How is it that You, being a Jew, ask me, a Samaritan woman, for a drink?" (For Jews have nothing to do with Samaritans.) [10]Jesus answered her, "If you knew [about] God's gift [of eternal life], and who it is who says, 'Give Me a drink,' you would have asked Him [instead], and He would have given you living water (eternal life)." [11]She said to Him, "Sir, You have nothing to draw with [no bucket and rope] and the well is deep. Where then do You get that living water? [12]Are You greater than our father Jacob, who gave us the well, and who used to drink from it himself, and his sons and his cattle also?" [13]Jesus answered her, "Everyone who drinks this water will be thirsty again. [14]But whoever drinks the water that I give him will never be thirsty again. But the water that I give him will become in him a spring of water [satisfying his thirst for God] welling up [continually flowing, bubbling within him] to eternal life."

*N*O ONE KNOWS her name, but her story is enlightening, life changing and memorable as this passage eternally defines the context of our spiritual worship. She came to the well that day as accustomed. By now the women of Sychar would have branded her for her debauchery, an eventuality of her infamy evident by their overt unceremonious avoidance. She walked alone to draw her water, maybe she saw him, maybe she didn't. Even if she did, her meeting with Jesus was no chance encounter and her conversation with Him would totally transform her life and the people of her entire community.

As Jesus looked at her, His eyes did not convey the judgment and scorn that was commonplace when she came into the public domain, but they were filled with compassion. He knew she needed so much more than the water she came to draw that could only satisfy her physical needs for a short while. Looking beyond her brazen façade into her heart He saw who she truly was, a helpless sinner that needed the Saviour. However, as He dialogued with her at first, her responses indicated that they were on two differing wavelengths. While they conversed about water, an obviously basic and vital element, the context held variant meanings to them both. Whereas she spoke to the need of the physical man, He addressed the greater need of the spiritual man, existent in every man.

Getting crossed signals in the simplest of conversation could happen relatively easy between two people if we don't understand the context. It gets more challenging if we misinterpret the spiritual connotation conveyed by the Holy Spirit at any given time, increasing our inclination towards misinterpretation. One might argue that at the time when Jesus ministered to this Samaritan woman she was a sinner and as such she lacked the spiritual understanding necessary to grasp

His ideology. While this is so, we would also find that such lack of understanding is also common among believers. Jesus oftentimes had to explain to His disciples, those who literally walked and talked with Him daily, the spiritual context of His words and redirect their traditional and cultural stereotyping. It is also quite possible for us to miss the heart of His message by fixating on the rigidity of religion and expecting God to speak or answer in conventional ways and manmade systemic forms.

Just like this social outcast, in the times when we do not quite grasp what the Master is saying and lack the discernment to see the bigger picture, we have the blessed opportunity for His presence to reveal it to us. We may also find that like her, when we understand His message, our focus totally shifts from the discomfiting situation generating the opportunity to meet with the Master. The momentous personal experience with His love and grace takes centre stage. Thankfully such an experience is not accessed or influenced by our class or nationality but by His unlimited compassion for lost sinners (Luke 19:10).

> **"...when we understand His message, our focus totally shifts from the discomfiting situation generating the opportunity to meet with the Master."**

We are truly blessed to know one so caring and merciful, the only one able to redirect the course of our lives by the revelation of His grace. He meets us right where we are, making no demands on us to change who we are in order to receive His love, except to believe in Him. But once we encounter the greatest love given to man from the Father above, we cannot doubt its overwhelming ability to give us peace and immediately recreate us into a child of the King. As revolting and guilty we think ourselves to be, He already knows that we need cleansing from the muck of sin and that's His job because only His blood qualifies to cleanse from sin. As you hear His voice today take a moment to understand the context of His communication and the purpose of His call. Our consequential spiritual awakening will definitely be life-changing.

Therefore if anyone is in Christ [that is, grafted in,
joined to Him by faith in Him as Savior], he is a new
creature [reborn and renewed by the Holy Spirit];
the old things [the previous moral and spiritual condition]
have passed away. Behold, new things have come
[because spiritual awakening brings a new life].
2 Corinthians 5:17 (Amplified Bible)

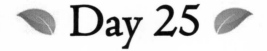# Day 25

Day 17
Blind Faith

Genesis 6:13–14 (New American Standard Bible)

[13]Then God said to Noah, "The end of all flesh has come before Me; for the earth is filled with violence because of them; and behold, I am about to destroy them with the earth. [14]Make for yourself an ark of gopher wood; you shall make the ark with rooms, and shall cover it inside and out with pitch.

Genesis 7:1–5

[1]Then the Lord said to Noah, "Enter the ark, you and all your household, for you alone I have seen to be righteous before Me in this time. [2]You shall take with you of every clean animal by sevens, a male and his female; and of the animals that are not clean two, a male and his female; [3]also of the birds of the sky, by sevens, male and female, to keep offspring alive on the face of all the earth. [4]For after seven more days, I will send rain on the earth forty days and forty nights; and I will blot out from the face of the land every living thing that I have made." [5]Noah did according to all that the Lord had commanded him.

*G*ENERALLY, WE ARE all ears and maybe even downright exuberant when receiving a direct word from the Lord, whether from His prophet or His Holy Spirit.

However, when the Lord gives us peculiar detailed instructions that require we cross the boundaries of common human comprehension, compounded by a visible structure that looks equally eccentric that is a totally different scenario. It is so much easier to obey God when we see the relevance of His directives to appreciate its application, but we may find ourselves questioning God when conversely, His instructions seem unconventional and well, absolutely ludicrous!

Rain.

It's a word that was probably non-existent before God used this term to categorise droplets of water from the heavens in His conversation with Noah. The simple reason is that until this watershed moment a mist rose up from the earth to water the ground (Genesis 2:6) ergo, precipitation had never ever been seen, or experienced anywhere by anyone. Additionally, no one, including Noah, had ever seen the earth covered by water and therefore, he had no reference to draw any comparison. To add insult to injury, he must have been attributed with even greater madness when the petting zoo cropped up near the ark's construction zone that cordoned off would-be passengers along with Noah and his family. But as God looked for a righteous man in that evil generation, it was only Noah He found (Genesis 6). He was the only man of faith whom God could use to build a massive flotation device that would become buoyant in a hypothetical flood created by imaginary rain.

Despite how foolish Noah knew he would have appeared to all the spectators he obeyed, holding fast to his faith in God and His word. He did not allow the expected criticisms and jeers of the masses to deter him or disrupt God's plan. He faithfully went each day to the construction site, painstakingly followed God's detailed blueprint for the ark and gathered the animals as instructed. Then the day finally arrived when the word of the Lord was fulfilled and suddenly, the oversized boat in the middle of nowhere made sense.

Although mixed emotions can sometimes greet the word of the Lord as we toggle between excitement and disdain in one fell swoop, the decision is wholly ours whether we choose to become the Noahs of our time, or not. We could decide to be obedient casting aside our fear of rejection, failure and ridicule, and go against the grain to fulfil His call. Or, we could allow that fear to cripple us into dodging our instructions and deposit us on the side-lines, swept up in the attack on those who dare to accept His mandate. But are you willing to chance disobedience to retain the favour of your peer group? Well, I encourage you to consider that like

> **❝...God called you to be His example of righteousness...by achieving the impossible through faith in Him and ultimately pointing others to His Son – Jesus, the Saviour.❞**

Noah, God called you to be His example of righteousness in this world by achieving the impossible through faith in Him and ultimately pointing others to His Son – Jesus, the Saviour.

Agreeably, the mission at hand may seem perplexing and beyond anything that we have attempted in the past, but instead of saying, *"Why me, Lord?"* why not change your tune to *"Why not me, Lord?"* So maybe it's beyond your current capacity, then trust God. Maybe it's beyond your understanding and comprehension, then believe God. Maybe it challenges your personal pride, then submit it to God. Do not be afraid of what lies ahead; hold fast to your faith in God and His word. When it comes to pass, and rest assured it will because God is not a man that He should lie (Numbers 23:19), you will be thankful that you were committed to the Master's call. Through faith and confidence in God's word, your single act of obedience will be the portal of blessings as an heir of righteousness. Trust God in all things and you will never be disappointed with your end result.

By faith [with confidence in God and His word] Noah,
being warned by God about events not yet seen, in
reverence prepared an ark for the salvation of his family.
By this [act of obedience] he condemned the world and
became an heir of the righteousness which comes by faith.
Hebrews 11:7 (Amplified Bible)

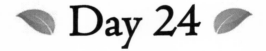 **Day 24**

Day 18
Success In Succession

Deuteronomy 31:7–8(Amplified Bible)

⁷Then Moses called to Joshua and said to him in the sight of all [the people of] Israel, "Be strong and courageous, for you will go with this people into the land which the Lord has sworn to their fathers to give them, and you will give it to them as an inheritance. ⁸It is the Lord who goes before you; He will be with you. He will not fail you or abandon you. Do not fear or be dismayed."

Joshua 1:1–2, 9

¹Now it happened after the death of Moses the servant of the Lord, that the Lord spoke to Joshua the son of Nun, Moses' servant (attendant), saying, ²"Moses My servant is dead; now therefore arise [to take his place], cross over this Jordan, you and all this people, into the land which I am giving to them, to the sons of Israel.

⁹Have I not commanded you? Be strong and courageous! Do not be terrified or dismayed (intimidated), for the Lord your God is with you wherever you go."

MOSES LOOKED OUT over the endless sea of faces that stood before him comprising Israel's twelve tribes poignantly aware that the time for implementing God's succession plan had come. His tenure as Israel's deliverer was at its climax, and his footprints would now be imprinted in the sands of a time gone by. God called him out of his wilderness refuge in Midian, placed him before Pharaoh, and used him to bring Israel out of Egypt by a mighty hand through the miraculous Red Sea crossing (Psalm 136:11-13). Moses was then entrusted with the law written by God's own finger on tablets of stone (Exodus 31:18) and finally brought Israel to the periphery of their Promised Land after a 40-year sanction for their murmurings (Numbers 14:34–35). However, his triumphant entry leading the millions that followed him out of Egypt was a riveting example of an anticlimactic end due to unrepentant anger.

Years earlier while leading the Israelites, Moses never envisioned that he would not be amongst them when they stood at the threshold of their final crossing, by way of the Jordan. This turn of events was initially unforeseen, but God's relationship with Moses was such that there was nothing hidden between them. Led by the Spirit of God in complete leadership style, he knew that the plan for succession was already in place. The Lord positioned Joshua in Moses' shadow, and it was there he learned first-hand about leadership and transitioned over time into the next leader that God desired for Israel (Deuteronomy 1:37-38). After 40 years of being an understudy, the day came for Joshua to take over the role.

God strategically immerses us in relationships with key persons that are specifically designed to influence and aid our character development while sharpening our skillset. These relationships are intended to help us grow spiritually, teaching us to exercise

> **"God strategically immerses us in relationships with key persons that are specifically designed to influence and aid our character development while sharpening our skillset."**

our faith in God as we gradually evolve to higher levels of leadership. We also see them demonstrating the importance of having a personal relationship with God and how we are to handle victories and deliverances as well as defeats and second chances. As we carefully observe our mentors, we would recognize that although they are not perfect, God uses them as instruments to fashion us into the individuals that He predestined us to become.

Our processing is always linked to a specific time and season for promotion when we must implement our learnings for the successful execution of our mandate. With the training wheels off and the mantle squarely on our shoulders, our eyes would transition from our predecessors to totally focus on the "...*Originator and Perfecter of our faith...*" (Hebrews 12:2 LEB). He would now guide and direct our every step, assuring us that we need not fear, doubt, and dismay because God will strengthen, retain and bear us up with His right hand of victory (Isaiah 41:10).

For the baton of faith to be effectively passed from one generation to the next until the blessed day of His coming, successorship is a must. In some regard, we are all a part of this process at differing stages and levels and to various degrees. Those that precede us at our workplace, in ministry, and life would one day place the baton they carry firmly into our hands, ultimately letting us know that the time has arrived for us to take our position at the helm. The encouragement Joshua received to be strong and relinquish fear would become our own and our state of readiness to move forward would be dependent on how we responded to His call.

I am convinced and confident like Paul that the work He began in us all He will continue to perfect and complete until Christ's return (Philippians 1:6). We may not know the date and time of our appointment to the next level of leadership or how it would come about, but God certainly does. It's already engraved in His plan for us. Let us therefore make good and godly choices about our future today by yielding to the Master's guided processing for progression. It's His guaranteed way for succession to be successful.

⁶"Be strong and brave, for you will be a successful leader
of my people; and they shall conquer all the land I promised
to their ancestors. ⁷You need only to be strong and courageous
and to obey to the letter every law Moses gave you, for if
you are careful to obey every one of them, you will be successful
in everything you do.
Joshua 1:6–7 (The Living Bible)

 # Day 23

Day 19
Purpose Precedes Primacy

Esther 4:10–14 (The Living Bible)

[10]Esther told Hathach to go back and say to Mordecai,
[11]"All the world knows that anyone, whether man or woman, who goes into the king's inner court without his summons is doomed to die unless the king holds out his gold scepter; and the king has not called for me to come to him in more than a month." [12]So Hathach gave Esther's message to Mordecai. [13]This was Mordecai's reply to Esther: "Do you think you will escape there in the palace when all other Jews are killed? [14]If you keep quiet at a time like this, God will deliver the Jews from some other source, but you and your relatives will die; what's more, who can say but that God has brought you into the palace for just such a time as this?"

Esther 5:1–2

[1]Three days later Esther put on her royal robes and entered the inner court just beyond the royal hall of the palace, where the king was sitting upon his royal throne. [2]And when he saw Queen Esther standing there in the inner court, he welcomed her, holding out the golden scepter to her. So Esther approached and touched its tip.

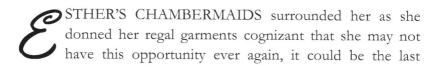 STHER'S CHAMBERMAIDS surrounded her as she donned her regal garments cognizant that she may not have this opportunity ever again, it could be the last

time. Nevertheless, the purpose that impelled her to make this unscheduled appearance before the king was greater than the possibility of her monarchical demise and likely execution. She was up against the one law that applied to everyone in the kingdom, and its enforcement was without exemption. Not even the queen, fairest in all the land and hand-picked by the king himself was guaranteed to test its precedency and escape unscathed.

As she made her way towards the palace, she must have recounted the conditions under which she, an orphaned Jewess, was grafted into Persia's royal dynasty. The infamy of her predecessor's impeachment wrought through her public defiance of the throne's sovereignty (Esther 1) may be about to have a repeat performance. Hence, her reign could end in comparable or even greater disgrace. Despite this knowledge, she prepared herself both spiritually and physically and embarked on her destined journey that would end before the king's throne. Accepting the potential conclusion to her boldness, she held on to her faith, believing God for a supernatural display of His changeless omnipotence in an expression of imperial favour.

> **66 For believers in Jesus Christ ... every appointment for advancement is the evidence of God's favour upon His children ...99**

In the world's system, promotion can be the reward of dedication, education and hard work intersected by opportunity. For believers in Jesus Christ, with or without the foregoing attributes, every appointment for advancement is the evidence of God's favour upon His children (Psalm 75:6–7) that becomes a platform for us to fulfil His ultimate purpose. Indeed, promotion can sometimes elevate our social status, position, and standard of living; but these benefits that we receive must not take precedence over the call of the Master. If we always view these advantages as privileges and blessings, then we may altogether avoid the pitfalls of pride and arrogance that emerge from the belief that we are entitled to them. As such, if a time comes when we must make seemingly detrimental decisions that threaten our status and popularity, we can humbly lay all the accolades of men aside if we truly desire to fulfil the will of God.

While we can monitor our progress through the pecking order of human systems, our purpose, position, and identity in God never change. We are always and forever will be His servants whom He would use to manifest His intrinsic glory in the earth (Colossians 1:27). Our obedience may come at a high price since elevation exposes us to increased public scrutiny that unmasks us before onlookers disclosing our secret affiliations, hidden allegiances, and private beliefs. However difficult and challenging the next move may seem, we can be encouraged by the knowledge that He is with us by His Holy Spirit. He protects and grants us favor among men that only the Master of our destiny can give. Up against the grimmest of outcomes, it is only our faith in El Elyon, the God Most High that can bring us through safely to the other side.

Esther proved her faith and declared her identity and true purpose when she entered the inner court of the king's palace. On that red-letter day, it was God's faithfulness that granted her the favour she received. When we walk in purpose, we are never alone or forsaken. He guides our way and provides the grace that we need to establish the authenticity of His call already evidenced by our faith and obedience. Do not take any move of His hand or elevation in your lives for granted; they can come and go at a moment's notice. See through the film of its glory to the heart of its purpose. He is preparing us for the next level of our journey when the honour we've received becomes an instrument to accomplish our destiny in Him. We have come into His kingdom of light (1 Peter 2:9) for such a time as this, let's make it count.

⁶For not from the east, nor from the west,
Nor from the desert comes exaltation.
⁷But God is the Judge;
He puts down one and lifts up another.
Psalms 75:6–7 (New King James Version)

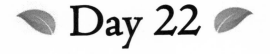 # Day 22

Day 20
Unscheduled Appointment

1 Samuel 17:45–48 (Amplified Bible)

[45]Then David said to the Philistine, "You come to me with a sword, a spear, and a javelin, but I come to you in the name of the Lord of hosts, the God of the armies of Israel, whom you have taunted. [46]This day the Lord will hand you over to me, and I will strike you down and cut off your head. And I will give the corpses of the army of the Philistines this day to the birds of the sky and the wild beasts of the earth, so that all the earth may know that there is a God in Israel, [47]and that this entire assembly may know that the Lord does not save with the sword or with the spear; for the battle is the Lord's and He will hand you over to us." [48]When the Philistine rose and came forward to meet David, David ran quickly toward the battle line to meet the Philistine. [49]David put his hand into his bag and took out a stone and slung it, and it struck the Philistine on his forehead. The stone penetrated his forehead, and he fell face down on the ground. [50]So David triumphed over the Philistine with a sling and a stone, and he struck down the Philistine and killed him; but there was no sword in David's hand.

I AM VERY CERTAIN THAT every believer would heave a soul-cleansing sigh of relief if the call of the Master came with an instruction manual, action plan or a *'To-Do List'* attached. Life would be so much easier wouldn't it? We would know what to do in every situation ridding ourselves of all the hullabaloo associated with uncertainty. But then, there would be no need for us to trust God or make ourselves available to hear from Him, develop relationship and fellowship with Him. Everything would become rote and remote, maybe even a little boring as well.

If we look at examples in the word, we would find instances where God's instructions were pointed such as Jonah's commission to Nineveh (Jonah 1:1–2) and the destruction of Jericho (Joshua 6:1–5). At other times God gives us the answer to our predicament with some details omitted as was the case when rival armies declared war against Judah during Jehoshaphat's reign (2 Chronicles 20). Even at other times, we see God bringing us to a place of impossibility and making a way where there is no way as exemplified with Israel's Red Sea crossing (Exodus 14). Then we come to incidences when no instruction as such is received, but by virtue of righteous indignation, individuals are propelled into action to destroy the works of the enemy. The latter was David's response to Goliath's defaming words against Israel's army that, by extension, defiled the God of Israel.

David's assignment began simple enough delivering food for his older brothers on the battlefront. Upon his arrival to the embankment, he immediately took note of the Philistine juggernaut who somehow believed that he could reprehensibly demoralize the armies of God without consequence. As he came within earshot of Goliath's verbal onslaught, his relationship with and reverence for God prohibited his silence.

He voiced his disgust in response to the scene he witnessed and received his brother's public castigation. But, giving no thought to the immense status of his opponent, David took the weaponry he was accustomed to and went out to combat with Goliath in the name of the LORD.

However, unlike the soldiers in Israel's infantry, God prepared him for this battle through unorthodox means; his training ground being the desert while taking care of humble sheep. David possibly thought he was protecting his helpless charges, but God was teaching him how to war fearlessly with his hands against vicious predators. In this solitude existence, his relationship with God deepened as evidenced by the psalms he penned, which encourage and strengthen us through our battles today. The encounter between these two

> **Every assignment and hurdle that comes our way is an occasion to declare the glory of the Lord and see His power manifested.**

unlikely opponents showcased what God had already established in David's life; quick response to the call of God regardless of the task and proclaiming victory by faith in the name of the Lord even before the actual battle takes place.

Nothing happens in the life of a believer by chance; even the remotest of encounters can become an opportunity for training and maybe even for battle. Every assignment and hurdle that comes our way is an occasion to declare the glory of the Lord and see His power manifested. There is absolutely no challenge too great for God to handle and no situation too far gone that God's intervention cannot change. Indeed, we could each be that unknown shepherd, employee, church worker or citizen fulfilling what begins as a mundane assignment that ultimately escalates into an all-out war cry against the kingdom of darkness declaring victory through the power of Almighty God, El Shaddai. As he stirs us into action, let us check our abilities at the gate and give Him free rein by our submission.

We won't always be aware of the details of each encounter. But as we assume our pre-battle position by abiding in God's presence, He has already prepared us for those unscheduled appointments to do battle with the enemy. From His vantage point, we are more than conquerors, and from ours, the battle is the Lord's. So let's move forward in faith and fearlessly engage in the battle that He has already won.

> For the Lord your God is He who goes with you,
> to fight for you against your enemies, to save you.
> **Deuteronomy 20:4 (Amplified Bible)**

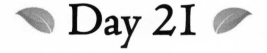

Day 21

Day 21
The Presence

Exodus 33:12–17 (New American Standard Bible)

[12]Then Moses said to the Lord, "See, You say to me, 'Bring up this people!' But You Yourself have not let me know whom You will send with me. Moreover, You have said, 'I have known you by name, and you have also found favor in My sight.' [13]Now therefore, I pray You, if I have found favor in Your sight, let me know Your ways that I may know You, so that I may find favor in Your sight. Consider too, that this nation is Your people." [14]And He said, "My presence shall go with you, and I will give you rest." [15]Then he said to Him, "If Your presence does not go with us, do not lead us up from here. [16]For how then can it be known that I have found favor in Your sight, I and Your people? Is it not by Your going with us, so that we, I and Your people, may be distinguished from all the other people who are upon the face of the earth?" [17]The Lord said to Moses, "I will also do this thing of which you have spoken; for you have found favor in My sight and I have known you by name."

*G*OD REVEALED HIS glory to both Moses and Israel through the miracles that permeated their journey from Egyptian bondage to Canaan's bounty. From the heart-stopping voice of God heard within the burning bush at Mount

Sinai, to the ten plagues that devastated Egypt, to Israel's inimitable deliverance through the parting of the Red Sea. It remains irrefutable; God Himself led Israel to freedom by His mighty hand (Deuteronomy 6:21; 26:8).

With each of these astonishing and extraordinary events and experiences, Israel's witness of God's glory and sovereignty was second to none. But Moses halted Israel's journey because there was still something more meaningful and desirable to him than the miracles he saw, the one constant that made it all possible. His desire was for God's presence to go with them as he recognized that this was the distinguishing factor that set Israel apart from every other people group on the earth. The presence of God defined their purpose, constituted their mantle of favour, and established the source of their strength; it was their be-all and end-all.

> **❝It is His presence in us that sets us apart in that we are no longer dependent on our own thoughts, philosophies, and strength to successfully navigate our lives.❞**

Living in the presence of God is as relevant today as it ever was for everyone who has accepted Jesus Christ as Lord and Saviour. In fact, through Christ, we have confident assurance that we abide in Him and He in us through the Holy Spirit's indwelling (1 John 4:13). It is His presence in us that sets us apart in that we are no longer dependent on our own thoughts, philosophies, and strength to successfully navigate our lives. These human attributes, though admirable and self-gratifying, are outshone in comparison to His presence that positions us to hear and be led by His voice in grace, love, and favour.

The more time we spend in His presence cultivating our relationship and communing with His Holy Spirit in submission and humility, the more we recognise how essential it is to our very existence. His pointed and clear instructions position us to successfully *"walk-out"* or rather live out our salvation daily with complete reliance on Him, eradicating our need for self-reliance (Philippians 2:12). Moses knew there was only one way he could manoeuvre through the hills and valleys of the journey that lay before him from the backside of the desert to the borders of their Promised Land. He knew that the presence of God would be an unending supply of grace to lead Israel, steer him toward the answers to every dilemma, and provide the right strategies to conquer their enemies.

God's presence enriches, empowers and equips us. We receive strength, comfort, and encouragement daily when we allow His presence to overshadow every area of our lives. The greatest challenge for us, however, is to remain focused on Him, especially with the distractions that would come to compete for our attention. Doubt, fear, anxiety, unbelief and frustration can quickly become a breeding ground for self-inflicted torture, rolling every conceivable negative possibility and its outcome around in our minds. They are all strategies in the enemy's plan to divert our attention and draw us out from His presence, making us vulnerable to spiritual attacks and a life of defeat. But we can rest in His grace that is sure and sufficient for us at every turn.

Looking unto God the Father through the righteousness of Jesus Christ, let us remain focused on being in His presence all day, every day. Challenge yourself today to make His presence a priority without which, like Moses, you refuse to go anywhere or do anything. Allow His presence to have an all-significant role in your life as He leads you forward to experience the promises that He has already set in place for each of us to enjoy. Make His presence your habitation and remember that as we lay our requests before Him, He will take charge of all things and grant us the peace that comes from resting in Him.

You will show me the path of life;
In Your presence is fullness of joy;
At Your right hand are pleasures forevermore.
Psalms 16:11 (Amplified Bible)

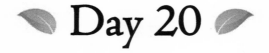 **Day 20**

Day 22
The Power Of Humility

1 Kings 3:7–13 (Amplified Bible, Classic Edition)

[7]Now, O Lord my God, You have made Your servant king instead of David my father, and I am but a lad [in wisdom and experience]; I know not how to go out (begin) or come in (finish). [8]Your servant is in the midst of Your people whom You have chosen, a great people who cannot be counted for multitude. [9]So give Your servant an understanding mind and a hearing heart to judge Your people, that I may discern between good and bad. For who is able to judge and rule this Your great people? [10]It pleased the Lord that Solomon had asked this. [11]God said to him, Because you have asked this and have not asked for long life or for riches, nor for the lives of your enemies, but have asked for yourself understanding to recognize what is just and right, [12]Behold, I have done as you asked. I have given you a wise, discerning mind, so that no one before you was your equal, nor shall any arise after you equal to you. [13]I have also given you what you have not asked, both riches and honor, so that there shall not be any among the kings equal to you all your days.

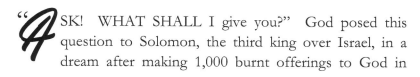

SK! WHAT SHALL I give you?" God posed this question to Solomon, the third king over Israel, in a dream after making 1,000 burnt offerings to God in worship earlier that day at Gibeon. What an immense responsibility it was to answer wisely to such a great opportunity! It was as if God presented Solomon with a blank cheque that He was guaranteed to honour, regardless of the request that he made. Whatever his response, the unchanging omnipotence of God would be immediately activated upon Solomon's life to bring it to pass. But of all the requests Solomon could have made of God, it was with a heart of humility that he voiced his deepest desire. He began by acknowledging God's greatness and confessed his insufficiencies and shortcomings as a leader. He then reflected on his role as Israel's king and asked for godly wisdom to lead God's people, not material wealth, military prowess, or state sovereignty. He desired supernatural discernment that would reflect the heart, mind and justice of God.

Every secular position that we attain and the resultant job titles we receive that become synonymous with our names have their importance. However, of even greater significance is recognizing that our secular positioning is God-ordained. He strategically places us within the marketplace, the world's system, to accomplish His purposes and

> **❝The true measure of a man's greatness is revealed when he is tested on how he perceives his own greatness.❞**

has intentionally designed each opportunity to showcase His power and glory through us. These appointments impact greatest when we can discern that they are more than mere opportunities for material gain and lifestyle preservation, but with them, humbly seek God to be guided by His call and achieve His will. His grace and favour always overshadow our abilities and achievements by enhancing our skills and miraculously opening doors that we can't on our own.

The true measure of a man's greatness is revealed when he is tested on how he perceives his own greatness. When God appointed Solomon as the successor to David's throne, he declared first and foremost that he was God's servant and petitioned Him for guidance. As a result of his selfless request that placed the needs of His people before his own, Solomon activated the release of godly blessings upon his life. God also covenanted with him that there would be no king to walk upon the face of the earth to compare with him in any domain or era.

Solomon inherited an immense task to rule a great nation. We may not all be called to such stately leadership, but we are called to be a witness of Jesus Christ. With this responsibility, we are required to showcase God's goodness through His amazing grace to those who are yet to experience it. We must remember that as God's servants, we must be ready to do as He instructs with the greatest of humility. Indeed, we may appear odd to observers, but our vision is greater than that which we can see with our eyes. It is cast beyond the material gains only relevant to this world and embraces the spiritual gains that have eternal value and advances His kingdom. But through our obedience to the call, just as He promised in His word, He will give us the desires of our heart and pour blessings upon us out of His immeasurable riches in glory in Christ Jesus (Philippians 4:19).

Solomon's response was supremely admirable on all levels, giving him access to treasures that are available to us right now.

When we make His kingdom our priority, we will see that He has already made our entire life His priority. Let us live like we know He is in control, because He is, and not become anxious but yield even our inabilities to Him. It's His plan that we are living out and by coming to terms with this truth, we free ourselves of its burden of proof. God is quite capable of doing that all by Himself.

> But first and most importantly seek (aim at, strive after) His kingdom and His righteousness [His way of doing and being right—the attitude and character of God], and all these things will be given to you also.
> **Matthew 6:33 (Amplified Bible)**

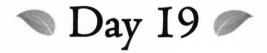

Day 19

Day 23
Predestined Allegiance

Ruth 1:8–10, 15–18 (Amplified Bible)

⁸But Naomi said to her two daughters-in-law, "Go back, each of you return to your mother's house. May the Lord show kindness to you as you have shown kindness to the dead and to me. ⁹May the Lord grant that you find rest, each one in the home of her husband." Then she kissed them [goodbye], and they wept aloud. ¹⁰And they said to her, "No, we will go with you to your people [in Judah]."

¹⁵Then Naomi said, "Look, your sister-in-law has gone back to her people and to her gods; turn back *and* follow your sister-in-law." ¹⁶But Ruth said, "Do not urge me to leave you or to turn back from following you; for where you go, I will go, and where you lodge, I will lodge. Your people will be my people, and your God, my God. ¹⁷Where you die, I will die, and there I will be buried. May the Lord do the same to me [as He has done to you], and more also, if anything but death separates me from you." ¹⁸When Naomi saw that Ruth was determined to go with her, she said nothing more.

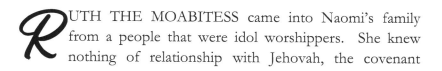

UTH THE MOABITESS came into Naomi's family from a people that were idol worshippers. She knew nothing of relationship with Jehovah, the covenant keeping God of her in-laws before her marriage, albeit she may have heard stories about His power and might. When the validity of their connection abruptly ended with the death of her husband, Ruth was no longer obligated to stay with Naomi, now a widowed childless matriarch having lost her own husband as well as her other son. She could have easily returned to Moab and reconnect with a familiar way of life, her people, family, and gods. But there was something she saw in Naomi that strongly influenced her otherwise, Ruth's desire to stay with her overriding any desire for the life she once knew. Her vehement insistence on leaving everything she knew behind to accompany Naomi back to Bethlehem forced the latter to concede.

Moving can be overwhelming; uprooting from familiar known paths to discover new territory and re-settle. It can be quite a difficult experience when the family structure is solid, but earth-shatteringly traumatic when you've lost loved ones that result in relocating. However, as we manoeuvre through these difficulties comforted and guided by the Holy Spirit, we may just find ourselves positioned to fulfil the call of God in ways we never anticipated. Naomi and Ruth both encountered loss through widowhood and there was no promise of a good life thereafter. But through her steadfast determination to follow Naomi, Ruth flowed directly into the perfect will of God for her life. Through Naomi's matchmaking instructions, her marriage to Boaz brought Ruth into the lineage through which Messiah, the Anointed One, would come.

None of us wish to experience loss. It's hard, an emotional rollercoaster that we all hope to avoid, but it is an inevitable part of life, difficult though it may be, that could leave us feeling

> **66 Through every difficulty that we face, we can draw strength from God's everlasting love, grace and mercy. 99**

empty, alone and embattled. Through every difficulty that we face, we can draw strength from God's everlasting love, grace and mercy. While for the moment the volatility of our situations may shake us to our very core, we can hold on to the promise that God will never leave nor forsake us (Deuteronomy 31:6, 8) and that He still has, and will always have the best in store for us, His beloved children. These two women were determined to make a fresh start against all the odds by embracing their uncertain future that lay ahead, but undoubtedly the call of God was fulfilled through their alliance and allegiance.

The Lord will bring people into our lives that form an integral part of the fulfilment of His ultimate plan. They would come alongside us as a coach preparing us to execute His will and purpose. By Ruth's example, we are encouraged to hold on to those persons that God has ordained to chaperone us. We will recognise them by their lifestyle, exhibiting character traits that reflect the inner workings of relationship with Christ. We will also experience changes in our own lives initiated by the example they provide for us to follow and the godly counsel that they give.

We need not fear the unknown for God is in control of our destiny, and He will provide all that we need to fulfil it. There is nothing that escapes His eye, and therefore, nothing we go through is unknown to Him. We only need to look beyond our present circumstances into His goodness, believing that all things, bitter and sweet, truly work out for our good. Of course, it may not always be as easy as we would prefer, it certainly wasn't for Ruth and Naomi. But the key is for us to trust Him unconditionally with the journey before us knowing that His Holy Spirit guides each step we take through the rough and rugged places and lands us right where we were always destined to be. Let's desire to be in the place that's our perfect fit by God's design.

And the Lord, He is the One who goes before you.
He will be with you, He will not leave you nor forsake you;
do not fear nor be dismayed."
Deuteronomy 3:8 (New King James Version)

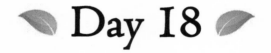

Day 18

Day 24
Grace At Lo-Debar

2 Samuel 9:3b–4; 7, 9–10 (Amplified Bible)

³And the king said, "Is there no longer anyone left of the house (family) of Saul to whom I may show the goodness and graciousness of God?" Ziba replied to the king, "There is still a son of Jonathan, [one] whose feet are crippled." ⁴So the king said to him, "Where is he?" And Ziba replied to the king, "He is in the house of Machir the son of Ammiel, in Lo-debar."

⁷David said to him, "Do not be afraid, for I will certainly show you kindness for the sake of your father Jonathan, and will restore to you all the land of your grandfather Saul; and you shall always eat at my table."

⁹Then the king summoned Ziba, Saul's servant, and said to him, "I have given your master's grandson everything that belonged to Saul and to all his house (family). ¹⁰You and your sons and your servants shall cultivate the land for him, and you shall bring in the produce, so that your master's grandson may have food to eat; but Mephibosheth, your master's grandson, shall always eat at my table."

ROM THE LUXURIOUS life he had in the palace where he played as a child with his father, Jonathan and grandfather, Saul hearing stories of David before he became king, Mephibosheth ended up a cripple in Lo-debar, a place of barrenness and desolation. He was an exile from his former life and believed that he was successfully hiding from the eyes of the reigning king. But, at the height of David's reign, the memory of his beloved friend and brother killed in battle propelled him to search for any surviving descendants of the house of Saul. He had hoped to show them God's grace and favour as a memorial to Jonathan.

So David's desire to find Mephibosheth was an offshoot of the brotherhood he shared with Jonathan. However, I am certain the inhabitants of Lo-debar were traumatized when the news broke that the king was looking for any remaining descendants of the former monarch. Filled with fear, Mephibosheth fell face down when he was brought before David. He was living a destitute life, although he originated from royalty, and up to now avoided drawing any attention to himself that would expose his existence and identity to the king. But with his efforts now thwarted, and his identity revealed he could no longer hide, and due to his physical condition, he could not run either. Little did he know that his life was about to be elevated from impoverishment to abundance through grace.

God's grace and favour is something that we did not deserve and simultaneously cannot earn but have been extended to us because of His extraordinary love through Jesus' sacrifice on the cross. If we take the time to recount incidences in our lives where we have received favour, we would realise that the hand of God has long been opening doors on our behalf, providing great blessings by His grace. He has indeed regarded our helpless estate and through His Son, made redemption available to us all. Through this grace, He created an avenue for us to leave our own Lo-debars behind littered with distress, frustration and our continuous attempts to make it through life without His presence. It really doesn't matter where we end up, whether we think our lot is deserved or sufficient. God's eyes are always upon us, and His grace can rescue all men from a spiritually destitute existence to dwell in and enjoy the presence of the King. At His table, we freely experience His love and favour, outfitted with His glory that has risen upon us (Isaiah 60:1).

> **"God's eyes are always upon us, and His grace can rescue all men from a spiritually destitute existence to dwell in and enjoy the presence of the King."**

Undeniably, it was grace that shook Lo-debar at its very foundation when it sought out Mephibosheth and today the grace of Jesus Christ seeks the lost and hopeless to transform man into a habitation for God. As recipients, we should be nothing short of compelled to showcase our gratitude through our worship and by our faithfulness and obedience to His voice. He has rescued us from physical and spiritual deprivation and impoverishment, giving us the necessary structure in His word to support our new way of life. We are now complete in Him as a joint heir with Jesus (Romans 8:15–17) and in His perfect likeness (1 John 4:17).

We are completely free from the chains of the past and the bondage of sin (Romans 6:14), redeemed and restored to fellowship with God, the Father (2 Corinthians 5:18). Let us look beyond the fear of being discovered by God's grace and shed that accusing guilty conscience that makes us insecure and vulnerable to Satan's attacks. Trust in the one who knows our beginning and our end; He loved us even while we were exiled from Him dwelling in the shame and disgrace that we falsely believed was all life could offer. Today through Christ, our Lo-debar existence has officially ended, and our new life of everlasting grace has begun.

> For the [remarkable, undeserved] grace of God
> that brings salvation has appeared to all men.
> **Titus 2:11 (Amplified Bible)**

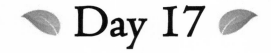# Day 17

Day 25
Providence

Genesis 37:23–24 (Amplified Bible)

[23]Now when Joseph reached his brothers, they stripped him of his tunic, the [distinctive] multicolored tunic which he was wearing; [24]then they took him and threw him into the pit. Now the pit was empty; there was no water in it.

Genesis 39:19–20

[19]And when Joseph's master heard the words of his wife, saying, "This is the way your servant treated me," his anger burned. [20]So Joseph's master took him and put him in the prison, a place where the king's prisoners were confined; so he was there in the prison.

Genesis 45:7–8

[7]God sent me [to Egypt] ahead of you to preserve for you a remnant on the earth, and to keep you alive by a great escape. [8]So now it was not you who sent me here, but God; and He has made me a father to Pharaoh and lord of all his household and ruler over all the land of Egypt.

THE LIFE OF JOSEPH is a classic example of sibling rivalry at its paradoxical worst and best. His brothers seized a great opportunity to once and for all be rid of the dreamer that plagued their existence with his superiority complex. Israel's blood flowed in all of their veins but everyone, including Joseph, knew that he was different and it constantly rattled their chains and unnerved the very fibre of their being. I am amazed at God's ways and that He can use anything, anyone and any situation to fulfil His plans, even destructive emotions like jealousy, anger, and hatred. Admittedly they turned Joseph's world upside down that fateful day and set him on a path of immense hardship and isolation. But all these negatives influenced an outcome that God always intended for Joseph and his entire family, especially the ones who wanted to destroy him.

Hated by his brothers who initially plotted his murder, and then flung into a pit, he was eventually fished out and sold into slavery recorded as the first victim of human trafficking. God's purpose brought him into Potiphar's house, a calm and balanced enough existence that was not intended to last and eventually wrecked by a lie. His resultant imprisonment placed him in yet another pit that still was not deep enough to keep him down or hold him back from achieving greatness. No attack against Joseph could destroy him or his dreams, and through his God-given ability to decipher their meaning, the time came for him to be ushered before Pharaoh to give a timely interpretation. By showcasing the divine spirit of God through his discernment and wise counsel, Pharaoh immediately entrusted Joseph with Egypt's complete governance.

Joseph's strategic positioning in Egypt was always where God intended for him to be, but the process was a fundamental part of his success. Yes, he encountered great difficulty and had some bitter experiences, but God used each challenge to refine his character and expose him to the Egyptian culture and lifestyle. His presence brought blessings upon Potiphar's house and in the prison. Under his leadership, blessings would also overtake Egypt turning them into the superpower assigned to preserve and sustain Abraham's lineage during the seven-year famine.

We are all just like Joseph in some regard as our purpose, mission and destiny have already been ordained and mapped out by Almighty God. Those challenges that we would wish away if we could, push us towards greater faith and deeper trust in God as we continue building relationship with Him. Throughout his dilemmas, Joseph held onto his God and the desire to be reunited

> **66Those challenges that we would wish away if we could, push us towards greater faith and deeper trust in God as we continue building relationship with Him.99**

with his beloved father. But through the series of events that preceded his heartfelt desire, he would realize the purpose for the hardships that he overcame, declaring that his suffering was all worth it in the end.

It is easy to think that we have a *"pit-calling"* or that *"it's just my luck"* when incessant difficulty comes at us from every direction. We may also consider that giving up the fight to overcome them may be easier than trusting God for breakthrough and believing His word for deliverance. However, whether we are in the pit of hopelessness or the dungeons of despair, there is one truth that holds fast: God's presence is in us and therefore, wherever we are, He's right there. His plans are greater than the difficulty we see before us, but we must choose whether we will stay the course until we see our purpose come to fruition or throw our hands up in defeat.

So yes, God has a purpose for us all and yes, His plans are good. He allows discomforts to come our way to encourage growth, strengthen us in difficulty, develop our character, and build our faith in Him. As we develop a greater understanding of His sovereignty in all things, let us walk in that faith, affirming His promised blessings through His word, knowing that His timing is always perfect. We too shall see the reason behind it all, and with grateful hearts, thank God that we answered His call.

And we know [with great confidence] that God [who is
deeply concerned about us] causes all things to work
together [as a plan] for good for those who love God, to
those who are called according to His plan and purpose.
Romans 8:28 (Amplified Bible)

Day 16

Day 26
Renewed Opportunities

John 5:1–9 (New American Standard Bible)

¹After these things there was a feast of the Jews, and Jesus went up to Jerusalem. ²Now there is in Jerusalem by the sheep gate a pool, which is called in Hebrew Bethesda, having five porticoes. ³In these lay a multitude of those who were sick, blind, lame, and withered, waiting for the moving of the waters; ⁴for an angel of the Lord went down at certain seasons into the pool and stirred up the water; whoever then first, after the stirring up of the water, stepped in was made well from whatever disease with which he was afflicted. ⁵A man was there who had been ill for thirty-eight years. ⁶When Jesus saw him lying there, and knew that he had already been a long time in that condition, He said to him, "Do you wish to get well?" ⁷The sick man answered Him, "Sir, I have no man to put me into the pool when the water is stirred up, but while I am coming, another steps down before me." ⁸Jesus said to him, "Get up, pick up your pallet and walk." ⁹Immediately the man became well, and picked up his pallet and began to walk.

THIS EVENT WAS A widely reported occurrence that was famous throughout the region. It drew the attention of many and was sought out by all that were infirmed in their hope of attaining a better quality of life.

The crowd of hopefuls was great, but the chance of healing exceedingly slim since only one person per season was eligible to receive their healing. Every cycle the race was on with the winner determined by timing, speed, and precision.

But there was one whose season of waiting seemed unending. He lacked the dexterity to strategically position himself to receive his miracle and, as a result, he became a perpetual casualty of lost opportunities. Up until this point all the likely candidates probably only knew of healing through this one method, from the angel and via the water. So when the opportunity to be healed by the Master came, he had no idea that he was speaking with the Healer Himself. Instead, his response echoed the despair of thirty-eight years rife with suffering without connecting to the question that only required a simple *"Yes, Lord"*.

Have you ever been asked a straightforward question like, *"What do you want?"* and instead of answering you try to explain why you do not have or cannot get what you want? Believe it or not, the response given by the lame man at Bethesda is more common in the church among believers than we think, reflecting the mind-set that we cannot receive from God unless we labour for it. But when we come into contact with the Master, there is only one response necessary, an honest one. We do not need to render an epistle that satisfies all the interrogatives because of our inability *'to do'*.

When Jesus came to this man, He knew everything about his condition and without assistance, there was no way he could ever reach the water first and receive his healing. Without the

Master, he may have remained right there for the rest of his life tormented by watching others come sick and leave well without the hope of being one of them. This reality is very relevant today as many of us could attest to feeling that we are on the side-lines waiting for our miracle while others pass us by with theirs in hand; the job, home, family and life they've always wanted. We can waste precious time grousing over the fact that we are as deserving as they are, and if we only got the opportunity they had, we will have what we want also. But Jesus is here to let us know that there is no need to compete to receive, we just have to believe (Mark 5:36, Luke 8:50).

When we place God's infinite ability to bless, heal and deliver in Jesus' name above the circumstances that hem us in, we acknowledge His sovereignty by submitting to His lordship and actually worship Him. As we speak the name of Jesus and declare His Word over our situation, we activate the realm of the supernatural and release the power of God to change every negative condition. We need not focus on what is happening around us but be steadfast in faith that our time of deliverance is present as long as we have Jesus, and by His very nature He is always ready to bless. Whatever your need is today, it is the desire of the Master for you to have it according to His will, and through His grace, we can receive it.

> **❝We need not focus on what is happening around us but be steadfast in faith that our time of deliverance is present as long as we have Jesus...❞**

As Jesus passes by your situation, know that He is there to bring permanent change. Also, know that He has no set pattern, so be open to receive His blessings through His method, known or not. Tune in to the voice of the Master and know that your time of deliverance has come. Don't miss it by trying to define it.

Bless and affectionately praise the Lord, O my soul,
And do not forget any of His benefits;
Who forgives all your sins, Who heals all your diseases;
Who redeems your life from the pit, Who crowns you
[lavishly] with Lovingkindness and tender mercy;
Who satisfies your years with good things,
So that your youth is renewed like the [soaring] eagle.
Psalm 103:2–5 (Amplified Bible)

Day 15

Day 27
Our True Treasure

Luke 7:44–50 (Amplified Bible)

[44]Then turning toward the woman, He said to Simon, "Do you see this woman? I came into your house [but you failed to extend to Me the usual courtesies shown to a guest]; you gave Me no water for My feet, but she has wet My feet with her tears and wiped them with her hair [demonstrating her love]. [45]You gave Me no [welcoming] kiss, but from the moment I came in, she has not ceased to kiss My feet. [46]You did not [even] anoint My head with [ordinary] oil, but she has anointed My feet with [costly and rare] perfume. [47]Therefore I say to you, her sins, which are many, are forgiven, for she loved much; but he who is forgiven little, loves little." [48]Then He said to her, "Your sins are forgiven." [49]Those who were reclining at the table with Him began saying among themselves, "Who is this who even forgives sins?" [50]Jesus said to the woman, "Your faith [in Me] has saved you; go in peace [free from the distress experienced because of sin]."

*I*T IS REMARKABLE HOW quickly we can shift gears from loving to judging; from basking in the love and grace of Jesus one moment to ridiculing a sinner for sin the next. Interestingly enough, the last time I checked I found out that sinners can't help it they actually sin, it's in their nature and before Jesus called me to receive His saving grace, I did as well. Thankfully shame-faced persons of notoriety, not the sanctimoniously self-righteous, are high on Jesus' priority listing as He searches out the lost sinners everywhere in need of redemption (Luke 19:10).

People may wonder about the authenticity of the call she received to minister to Jesus in such a peculiar eyebrow-raising manner on account of her reputation. She left her home duty-bound to see the Master with her precious treasure worth a fortune in hand. Conscious of His predominantly public ministry, the chance that the ceremonial obligation she was about to perform would be away from public scrutiny was unlikely. In fact she knew Jesus' visit to Simon's house, a Pharisee, would constitute the presence of other Pharisees and also that His chosen 12 would be close. With her history in the public domain, there was no way that she could sidestep the shame of her past at this pious gathering, but the call to anoint the Master's feet was greater than their judgment.

Braving the humiliation, she obeyed the call and received the grace of the Saviour. Jesus' words to the crowd shielded her from their reprehension, and with nothing further to lose, she displayed selfless devotion to the Master by honouring Him where His host had utterly failed, in a most unorthodox manner. Simon showed his esteemed visitor no traditional courtesies and condemned her for doing so before the entire company. Through her broken spirit and contrite heart, her reverence and sacrificial worship (Psalm 51:17) honoured the Master, and she received His unconditional love and forgiveness in return. She left Simon's house that day finally free from the bondage of sin.

So here is the question that Jesus' response begs of each of us; are we honouring Him with our sincere love and devotion? Have we become ritualistic and smug with the treasure of grace that He shed His precious blood for us to receive freely? We have to accept the fact that a life of dedication to Him may not always receive the favour or approval of men. There may also be times when we may not even understand the significance of the Holy Spirit's instructions or know the results our submission would yield, but He does.

Our place is not to judge but to do the will of the Lord. Those in closest proximity to Jesus were furthest from comprehending this scene that they witnessed which fully endorsed the ultimate purpose of the Messiah. They focused on the past sins of the woman without recognizing His amazing grace and power to deliver a vile prostitute from sin, which they also needed. As we stand in His presence, let us not only be physically present to speak His name casually but be spiritually alert to the power that it holds and the salvation that He brings to all who accept Him as Saviour.

> **66 ...the King of Kings does not need our earthly treasures, but as we willingly pour them out at His feet, we become available to receive His grace, the real treasure in our earthen vessels. 99**

Only then would we see that the King of Kings does not need our earthly treasures, but as we willingly pour them out at His feet, we become available to receive His grace, the real treasure in our earthen vessels.

Many would have witnessed her redemption without remorse for their own sin as they misguidedly believed that they were exempt from the need for the Saviour by their acts of self-righteousness. Well my friend, we cannot become righteous except through Christ, the only one who can save us from our sins (Acts 4:12). Jesus' words confirmed to all that He has the power to wipe them all away and keep us free from its entanglement when we receive His treasure of grace. If you haven't received it as yet, then this is your opportunity. Welcome His grace into your life and see for yourself that it's the best decision you can ever make. Receive it today.

[23]since all have sinned and continually fall short of the glory of God, [24]and are being justified [declared free of the guilt of sin, made acceptable to God, and granted eternal life] as a gift by His [precious, undeserved] grace, through the redemption [the payment for our sin] which is [provided] in Christ Jesus,
Romans 3:23–24 (Amplified Bible)

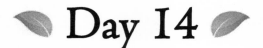

Day 14

Day 28
The Righteousness Stand

Daniel 3:24–27 (Amplified Bible)

²⁴Then Nebuchadnezzar the king [looked and] was astounded, and he jumped up and said to his counselors, "Did we not throw three men who were tied up into the midst of the fire?" They replied to the king, "Certainly, O king." ²⁵He answered, "Look! I see four men untied, walking around in the midst of the fire, and they are not hurt! And the appearance of the fourth is like a son of the gods!" ²⁶Then Nebuchadnezzar approached the door of the blazing furnace and said, "Shadrach, Meshach, and Abed-nego, servants of the Most High God, come out [of there]! Come here!" Then Shadrach, Meshach, and Abed-nego came out of the midst of the fire. ²⁷The satraps, the prefects, the governors and the king's counselors gathered around them and saw that in regard to these men the fire had no effect on their bodies—their hair was not singed, their clothes were not scorched or damaged, even the smell of smoke was not on them.

THREE CAPTIVES IN a foreign idolatrous land were brought before the king to answer for their insolence and treason by their decision not to bow to his newly minted golden image. Their devout reverence for Jehovah God did not permit them to worship any other god, even if it was the only way for their lives to be preserved. They were defiant in their decision yet respectable in their riposte when called to the chambers of the Babylonian monarch for disobeying his decree to worship the image. Unaffected by the penalty for their choice, to be thrown into a raging fire without any assurance of deliverance, they were steadfast in their righteous stand. They placed their confidence in the God of Israel and His omnipotence and regardless of the outcome, their resolve remained. Whether at present or in the future, whether for a favour or salvation, they would not bow.

I'm certain that we have all encountered at least one *'do or die'* dilemma where conformance was rampant. Such situations are quite prevalent in the marketplace where one's actions and statements can be often and easily ridiculed because of a personal relationship with Jesus, the Master. For this stand, we may have to face our own fiery furnaces of misrepresentation, victimisation, slander or just pure hatred. Our decision to go against the grain can sever relationships, distort the lines of communication, and destroy hope for the future. It is not always easy to make a public stand knowing that you would be ostracised for it, but all believers have a responsibility to destroy everything exalted and erected against the true knowledge of the living God (2 Corinthians 10:5).

Honestly, our way of life in response to the call of God is no secret to those around us. These three Hebrews were known for their heritage and lifestyle since their arrival in Babylon and they had no equal when it came to job performance which caught the king's attention very early in their career (Daniel 1:19–20). Their open commitment to a godly lifestyle gnawed away at their cohorts and a *'golden'* opportunity presented itself to finally wipe these foreigners out from the king's employ. How easy it would have been for them to shelve their convictions this one time to show their allegiance to the king and be accepted by their peers. However, they refused to discuss the matter declaring that their allegiance was to Jehovah God, and Him only. They probably knew that they had been set up by their associates anyway.

Today our world is filled with compromise, even amongst believers. Many practices that contravene the word of God have become widely accepted and publicly supported while truth is chipped away and righteousness is increasingly ignored and rejected. The unpopularity of being called to live a separated life has transcended time, but our commitment to being steadfast in our faith in Christ and stand for His truth remains. Indeed, while Jesus walked the earth He was hated for the truth that He spoke, He also admonished us that we would be partakers and recipients of this hatred for representing that truth in His name (John 15:18–25).

> **❝Our bold stand for righteousness may not be popular, but we can only do so by faith in Him, and to stand for Him is to stand for the highest truth that exists.❞**

Our bold stand for righteousness may not be popular, but we can only do so by faith in Him, and to stand for Him is to stand for the highest truth that exists. As we continue to stand firm in the liberating grace of Christ (Galatians 5:1), we must remember that we are no longer slaves to the dictates of this world's system, its idols, and the conflicting ideologies that they support. As you assume your position, stand firm and relentless, despite whatever attacks may come your way, the presence of the one standing in the fire with you will be undeniable. He promises to strengthen and empower us when we are deserted and rescue us from all evil attacks, both now and forever. Trust the Master as you stand for truth, there is nothing you have to lose, but everything to gain in His heavenly kingdom.

The Lord will rescue me from every evil assault, and
He will bring me safely into His heavenly kingdom;
to Him be the glory forever and ever. Amen.
2 Timothy 4:18 (Amplified Bible)

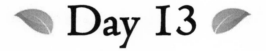

Day 13

Day 29
Majority Rule

2 Kings 6:15–17 (Amplified Bible)

¹⁵The servant of the man of God got up early and went out, and behold, there was an army with horses and chariots encircling the city. Elisha's servant said to him, "Oh no, my master! What are we to do?" ¹⁶Elisha answered, "Do not be afraid, for those who are with us are more than those who are with them." ¹⁷Then Elisha prayed and said, "Lord, please, open his eyes that he may see." And the Lord opened the servant's eyes and he saw; and behold, the mountain was full of horses and chariots of fire surrounding Elisha. ¹⁸When the Arameans came down to him, Elisha prayed to the Lord and said, "Please strike this people (nation) with blindness." And God struck them with blindness, in accordance with Elisha's request. ¹⁹Then Elisha said to the Arameans, "This is not the way, nor is this the city. Follow me and I will lead you to the man whom you are seeking." And he led them to Samaria.

*I*MAGINE AN ENTIRE army being sent to seize one man! One would think that this move by the Syrian king was a waste of resources, but he knew that Elisha was no ordinary man because he served an extraordinary God. It would have taken an army to seize him, if it was possible at all. Elisha was the renowned Prophet in Israel who advised King Jehoram of God's instructions regarding godliness, matters of state, and military preparedness. When God revealed that the Syrian army planned an ambush against Israel in a specific place, Elisha wasted no time to inform the king who immediately took the necessary precautions. The next ambush was set at Dothan to abduct Elisha, the thorn in their side and primary source of Syria's woes.

A very plausible question would be, why didn't God warn Elisha of Syria's new plot against him the way He revealed their plan to ambush Israel? I know sometimes we wonder about the entrapments and snares that the enemy has set up against us in our homes, in ministry, and on our jobs, and we question God, *"Why wasn't this attack of the enemy revealed to me?"* We may think that foreknowledge of the enemy's schemes would ensure that we have the upper hand in battle strategically. This approach may be beneficial to us in some regard, but there is a danger that we could inadvertently lose sight of God's greater plan for us to live by faith and to trust Him.

When Elisha received the report regarding his would-be captors, he gave no chorus to the initial lament of despair by confessing or conceding to what his servant saw with his physical eyes. With confident trust in Jehovah Sabaoth, his response was one of faith knowing that there was a purpose to the Syrian army's encircling of Dothan because God allowed it. Instead, he focused on the higher authority of the supernatural realm where the real battle takes place, even right now.

From the moment God calls us and we begin walking in His will we automatically become enemy targets. When we submit to

His sovereignty and proclaim His word our faith in Him changes our perspective, and by trusting in Him for intervention and salvation, we can even impact the people around. As a result, we would identify two distinct groups of people within our purview. One group would be grateful for the message of truth and willingly submit to the Master's call and His plans. But to the other group, we would be an offence because that same truth unmasks their hidden agendas to destroy His plans and those whom He called to fulfil them. So while we would be welcomed and embraced by some, others would reject and target us for destruction, but God's faithfulness shall always prevail.

We are given a very detailed description of the heavenly armies of Jehovah Sabaoth, the Lord of Hosts through Elisha's prayer of reassurance for his servant. This revelation confirms that even when confronted by physical opposition the spiritual realm remains superior. God does not only give us the upper hand but He also gives us victory over enemy attacks, and like Elisha, we are empowered to redirect the works of darkness away from us

> **66... through the finished work of Jesus Christ on the cross, we have been delivered from every work of darkness and are triumphant over every evil attack that comes our way.99**

altogether. Today, through the finished work of Jesus Christ on the cross, we have been delivered from every work of darkness (Colossians 1:13) and are triumphant over every evil attack that comes our way (Colossians 2:15).

It may appear to onlookers that we stand and fight alone, but the army of God always stands with us and for us. He reminds us that the battle isn't ours, it's His (2 Chronicles 20:15) and we are required to trust and believe in Him and His power, not ours (Deuteronomy 20:4). Despite how ominous the battle may appear based on what we see taking place around us, we know that our God is greater and mightier than those that are against us. As you look at your troubling circumstances, take courage and by faith, receive the abiding victory that Jesus has already provided for you. He has already overcome the troubles of this world and in Him we shall have perfect peace.

I have told you these things, so that in Me you may have [perfect] peace. In the world you have tribulation and distress and suffering, but be courageous [be confident, be undaunted, be filled with joy]; I have overcome the world."
[My conquest is accomplished, My victory abiding.]
John 16:33 (Amplified Bible)

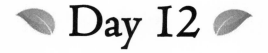

Day 12

Day 30
Synchronised Calling

Acts 9:10–17 (New American Standard Bible)

[10]Now there was a disciple at Damascus named Ananias; and the Lord said to him in a vision, "Ananias." And he said, "Here I am, Lord." [11]And the Lord said to him, "Get up and go to the street called Straight, and inquire at the house of Judas for a man from Tarsus named Saul, for he is praying, [12]and he has seen in a vision a man named Ananias come in and lay his hands on him, so that he might regain his sight." [13]But Ananias answered, "Lord, I have heard from many about this man, how much harm he did to Your saints at Jerusalem; [14]and here he has authority from the chief priests to bind all who call on Your name." [15]But the Lord said to him, "Go, for he is a chosen instrument of Mine, to bear My name before the Gentiles and kings and the sons of Israel; [16]for I will show him how much he must suffer for My name's sake." [17]So Ananias departed and entered the house, and after laying his hands on him said, "Brother Saul, the Lord Jesus, who appeared to you on the road by which you were coming, has sent me so that you may regain your sight and be filled with the Holy Spirit."

THE LORD CALLED TWO persons in this event that altered church history, and initially, they both had immensely divergent views regarding the teachings of the Lord Jesus Christ. While Saul was committed to destroying all believers that followed Jesus, Ananias was already a convert, fully aware of Saul's *'holy'* campaign to annihilate believers everywhere in his stout-hearted attempt to expunge this *'new'* gospel. If Saul had the opportunity to carry out his plans both men would have met under very different circumstances. But amidst the escalating crisis of martyrdom among the saints of the early church, starting with Stephen (Acts 8:1), the Lord Jesus intervened in a supernatural way along Saul's journey. His plans were immediately halted by a call that questioned his persecution of Christ (Acts 9:4–5), while Ananias, a believer amid those earmarked for destruction, was called to minister to this *'godly'* mercenary.

God's instructions to both parties were quite simple, yet to Ananias, under the prevailing conditions, this simple instruction was a most difficult mind-boggling task. We might mirror his distress and uncertainty if we were instructed by God to go and minister to someone who hates us, literally to death, and more so the one whom we represent. However, we must first recognize that when God calls us, His plan for us in already set in motion and only awaits our obedience. Second, although the task can appear simultaneously dangerous and terrifying, we can seek the Lord for His divine guidance, empowerment, and favour. Lastly, as we obey, we must also walk in faith as His ambassadors through whom He will move and speak. Any opposition we face is therefore not against us per se, but against God and His perfect will.

Saul began his journey to Damascus without any foreknowledge of God's real purpose for his life; that he was called to champion this same gospel of Jesus Christ that he was working so diligently to abolish. In preparation for the terror about to descend upon the believers in Damascus, Ananias did not anticipate this miraculous turn of events in which he would play a significant role. Neither of them knew that their encounter would be a pivotal moment in the revelation of the church as the body of Christ, and the eternal impact of the gospel on all humanity.

Our instructions from God must not be taken casually, seen as insignificant, or treated with scant courtesy, even if we believe that following them will not end well for us or that it should be someone else's responsibility. As much as we would like to, we cannot foreknow every detail of our role in the fulfilment of God's plan or how our response will alter our own lives and maybe even the course of history. However, every

> **66However, every call is interwoven into God's higher purpose that through Christ, all people have the opportunity to be reconciled unto Him.99**

call is interwoven into God's higher purpose that through Christ, all people have the opportunity to be reconciled unto Him (2 Corinthians 5:18–20). It was for this purpose that Jesus was made the ultimate sacrifice for sin, and we are commissioned to fulfil His call and bear His witness to others (Matthew 28:19–20; Mark 16:15–16).

Through Ananias' obedience, he witnessed Saul's conversion from darkness to become a follower of Jesus Christ first-hand. We read about him in the Bible, renamed Paul, as the one who instructed the early church, guiding the believers into Christian maturity by establishing God-breathed principles in his epistles that continue to guide believers everywhere. Let us not even think of where the church would be today if Ananias disobeyed the call of God or what position you or I would be in if we responded in kind. Let us, however, be committed to fulfilling the Master's call and walk worthy of it by understanding that through our obedience, this gospel of salvation will continue to penetrate the darkness of this world and give all who would believe new life in Christ. It's the best way to demonstrate our gratitude and thankfulness for redemption.

So I, the prisoner for the Lord, appeal to you to live a life
worthy of the calling to which you have been called
[that is, to live a life that exhibits godly character, moral courage,
personal integrity, and mature behavior—a life that expresses
gratitude to God for your salvation],
Ephesians 4:1 (Amplified Bible)

Day II

Day 31
Placed In His Service

1 Timothy 1:12–19 (New American Standard Bible)

[12]I thank Christ Jesus our Lord, who has strengthened me, because He considered me faithful, putting me into service, [13]even though I was formerly a blasphemer and a persecutor and a violent aggressor. Yet I was shown mercy because I acted ignorantly in unbelief; [14]and the grace of our Lord was more than abundant, with the faith and love which are found in Christ Jesus. [15]It is a trustworthy statement, deserving full acceptance, that Christ Jesus came into the world to save sinners, among whom I am foremost of all. [16]Yet for this reason I found mercy, so that in me as the foremost, Jesus Christ might demonstrate His perfect patience as an example for those who would believe in Him for eternal life. [17]Now to the King eternal, immortal, invisible, the only God, be honor and glory forever and ever. Amen. [18]This command I entrust to you, Timothy, my son, in accordance with the prophecies previously made concerning you, that by them you fight the good fight, [19]keeping faith and a good conscience, which some have rejected and suffered shipwreck in regard to their faith.

WHATEVER WE WERE before we met the Master, we no longer are afterward. By accepting Jesus Christ as the Son of God and His sacrifice for our sin, He instantly transforms our state of being. Physically we look the same, but we are new creatures; reborn and recreated spiritually not rehabilitated or refurbished (2 Corinthians 5:17). We would experience a gradual character transformation evident through changes in our mindsets, habits, and behaviour by yielding to the indwelling Holy Spirit. As we allow Him to become our spiritual compass, as it were, He synchronizes our spirit from within to exhibit that of Christ's. He remodels our thoughts to focus on things that are excellent and worthy of praise (Philippians 4:8) and enables us to make decisions that reflect godliness (1 Timothy 4:7). He even transforms our speech to proclaim life and strength that will bless all who hear our words (Ephesians 4:29).

Before his encounter with the Master and the resultant call he received to carry His gospel, Paul ignorantly believed that he was doing what was required of him as a Pharisee. He was convinced that by persecuting Christians he was honouring God. But after his experience on the Damascus road, his life and perspective on the gospel were dramatically changed. From a violent adversary of this new doctrine of Christ, God appointed Paul to become one of its chief heralds after his conversion.

In Paul's admonition to Timothy, he acknowledged first and foremost that although sincere in his pursuit of truth, he was sincerely wrong and ignorant in his belief. He pointed out that it was only by the mercy and grace of Jesus Christ he was afforded an opportunity to receive eternal life. He professed his gratitude to the Lord, humbled that he was found worthy to be placed in His service despite his widely publicized transgressions while he was a sinner. Though he endured much physical abuse and suffering himself as a result of spreading the gospel of Christ (2 Corinthians 11:23–27), he was contented to be doing the Master's will, boasting in his weaknesses to showcase the glory of God's strength at work in his life (2 Corinthians 12:10).

It is only by the work of the Holy Spirit in us that we are called and placed into service for the Master, there is no other way. As believers, our primary focus must be to seek His perfect will for our lives and to follow His written and spoken instructions accordingly. Additionally, we must recognize that in His service, wherever He positions us and whatever we are to do, it is all about fulfilling His purpose (Philippians 2:13). Our status, according to the world's lenses, does not define us as we are called to serve at all levels, and our service is primarily unto Him. We need not be motivated by satisfying man's expectations of us. As we fulfil our service unto God, we will automatically fulfil and surpass human targets and exceed their parameters. They may not be able to understand why or how and even hate us for it, but like Daniel, God's excellent spirit in us will produce a life of excellence (Daniel 5:11–12).

> **"As we fulfil our service unto God, we will automatically fulfil and surpass human targets and exceed their parameters."**

Being called from darkness into His marvellous light (1 Peter 2:9), and by extension His service is not an entitlement. It is a privilege and an honour that should not be taken lightly with a mandate that we cannot fulfil anywhere else except in His perfect will. There are situations awaiting our attention and intervention, people who are awaiting the ministry that God has birthed within us, and blessings to be poured out upon us through His divine favour and goodness.

I know that it is human nature to be a bit unsettled when we are unable to see the entire plan unfold all at once, but what matters is that we say yes to His call and free ourselves to trust Him unconditionally. In His service, our fulfilment of even the simplest directives has great worth, continually manifesting God's purpose for our lives as we walk in obedience. Christ already gave us the example to follow and His word assures us that as we serve Him, the Father will honour us. We have everything we need right before us, so let's choose wisely.

If anyone serves Me, he must [continue to faithfully] follow Me [without hesitation, holding steadfastly to Me, conforming to My example in living and, if need be, suffering or perhaps dying because of faith in Me]; and wherever I am [in heaven's glory], there will My servant be also. If anyone serves Me, the Father will honor him.
John 12:26 (Amplified Bible)

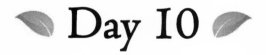 # Day 10

Day 32
Your 100%

Matthew 25:20–28 (New King James Version)

[20]"So he who had received five talents came and brought five other talents, saying, 'Lord, you delivered to me five talents; look, I have gained five more talents besides them.' [21]His lord said to him, 'Well done, good and faithful servant; you were faithful over a few things, I will make you ruler over many things. Enter into the joy of your lord.' [22]He also who had received two talents came and said, 'Lord, you delivered to me two talents; look, I have gained two more talents besides them.' [23]His lord said to him, 'Well done, good and faithful servant; you have been faithful over a few things, I will make you ruler over many things. Enter into the joy of your lord.'

[24]"Then he who had received the one talent came and said, 'Lord, I knew you to be a hard man, reaping where you have not sown, and gathering where you have not scattered seed. [25]And I was afraid, and went and hid your talent in the ground. Look, there you have what is yours.' [26]"But his lord answered and said to him, 'You wicked and lazy servant, you knew that I reap where I have not sown, and gather where I have not scattered seed. [27]So you ought to have deposited my money with the bankers, and at my coming I would have received back my own with interest. [28]Therefore take the talent from him, and give it to him who has ten talents.

*M*ORE OFTEN THAN we would like to believe, talented people bury their abilities to safeguard against responsibility, accountability and hard work. Think about what our world would be like today if Thomas Edison gave up after his first failed attempt to create a commercial light bulb, if Beethoven did not prefer to compose his own music or if Walt Disney decided that the naysayers were right about his dream to build a theme park. These men changed the landscape of modern convenience, music and entertainment by a willingness to push beyond the set boundaries of their time and use their talent to realise their dreams.

God has entrusted each of us with specific talents. It is interesting that in the parable Jesus gave He would use talent in the context of money, something of worth that can either appreciate or depreciate. It is also noteworthy that the talents were not distributed "*equally*" in terms of quantity as the amount each servant received varied. But for each individual, their allotment was their 100 percent and they were required to work with the amount assigned, to invest and increase accordingly.

Jesus showed that among the three servants, there was one that did not care for his assignment, who found that their master expected too much from him. With this skewed perspective, he made no attempt to utilise his talent while the others doubled theirs. Far too often we find that people are more willing to bury what God has invested in them because it takes too much effort to develop it and put it to work for His honour and glory. We may even find that some people become defunct with their godly investments because they unwisely compare theirs with others (2 Corinthians 10:12) and covet what seems to be a better assignment. But for those that head in this direction with God's treasure, they deny themselves the opportunity for self-development and to be enriched spiritually according to God's purpose and reinvest in His kingdom.

Every ability, talent and gifting that God has entrusted into our stewardship is designed and intended for our growth and development. It's not a means for God to utilize spare resources and keep us on our toes, it is actually beneficial for us. As we allow the Holy Spirit to influence our decisions regarding each deposit, He equips us to serve in a higher capacity with our 100 percent ever increasing. Where the Lord places us and how much He invests in us is immaterial as there is no hierarchy of better or worse with His investments. We are, therefore, mandated to develop them to the best of our ability and do all that we can for the Master, and ourselves, with what He has given us.

> **"Every ability, talent and gifting that God has entrusted into our stewardship is designed and intended for our growth and development."**

Jesus declared that the two servants who submitted to the master's plan were able to increase their investment and capacity for service, for which they were blessed. For the servant who refused to work and defiantly buried his treasure, stating that his great fear of the master was the reason why, a series of negative occurrences ensued. First, the talent he received depreciated as during the time it was in his possession the talents of the others doubled in value. Second, he lost an opportunity for personal development and consequently, with no added skillset to showcase, his worth depreciated. Lastly, because of fear and a lazy spirit, he lost the trust of his master and his position of honour.

You are already equipped to multiply whatever God has invested in you. It may seem challenging and appear insignificant, but nothing is too much or too little to do for the Master of our destiny. Do not look at the portfolio of another and focus 100 percent on your mandate. As we apply His wisdom, He will increase us, adding blessing upon blessing to the humble servant that understands His purpose is made perfect through the grace that He gives to all.

> "For to everyone who has [and values his blessings and gifts from God, and has used them wisely], more will be given, and [he will be richly supplied so that] he will have an abundance; but from the one who does not have [because he has ignored or disregarded his blessings and gifts from God], even what he does have will be taken away.
> **Matthew 25:29 (Amplified Bible)**

 # Day 9

Day 33
Humility Exalted

1 Corinthians 1:26–31 (Amplified Bible)

²⁶Just look at your own calling, believers; not many [of you were considered] wise according to human standards, not many powerful or influential, not many of high and noble birth. ²⁷But God has selected [for His purpose] the foolish things of the world to shame the wise [revealing their ignorance], and God has selected [for His purpose] the weak things of the world to shame the things which are strong [revealing their frailty]. ²⁸God has selected [for His purpose] the insignificant (base) things of the world, and the things that are despised and treated with contempt, [even] the things that are nothing, so that He might reduce to nothing the things that are, ²⁹so that no one may [be able to] boast in the presence of God. ³⁰But it is from Him that you are in Christ Jesus, who became to us wisdom from God [revealing His plan of salvation], and righteousness [making us acceptable to God], and sanctification [making us holy and setting us apart for God], and redemption [providing our ransom from the penalty for sin], ³¹so then, as it is written [in Scripture], "He who boasts and glories, let him boast and glory in the Lord."

OXYMORONS ARE often the origin of many a quandary that leaves us a tad more perplexed that we tend to appreciate. Some may have great difficulty accepting the context of this theme presented by Paul where the foolish, weak and insignificant denounce the wise, strong and powerful. Some may even take offense to the former receiving higher honour when we all prefer for it to be given to the latter, reflecting a standard to which we aspire both openly and secretly. Who would be desirous of being despised as a result of deliberate humility, and how could this lowliness establish anyone's calling and completely glorify God? Why not just use our God-given abilities to work out a brilliant plan to execute the call of God as is within our power to do?

Let's face it, humility is as unpopular as a canker sore these days. Exhibiting this character trait would entail subscribing to the fact that there is actually a complete supernatural plan bigger than ours that God has called us to walk in. The greatest example of humility is the plan of salvation through Jesus Christ, freely available to everyone, irrespective of our social or financial status. His agonizing and sacrificial death on the cross that qualifies us to be clothed in His righteousness and made acceptable to God remains a foolish principle to the many that reject it. Our sanctification, only accessible through His grace that sets us apart to fulfil the Master's call, therefore, becomes grossly unpalatable to those who believe that human effort must be a part of the equation of success.

> **66The greatest example of humility is ... salvation through Jesus Christ, freely available to everyone, irrespective of our social or financial status.99**

For all those accepting Jesus as Saviour and His finished work on the cross, Paul readily points out that if they were measured by human standards they would never have qualified to be called by God. Moreover, the perception that we can earn our righteousness is simultaneously dispelled in that, we can only be made righteous through Christ and only God could be credited for us receiving this gift. He has favoured us through His plan of salvation to receive the ultimate blessing once lost to man, a reconciled relationship with God.

From the time Paul wrote this letter to the Corinthian church up to today, the message of salvation continues to be a stumbling block for those who cannot logically comprehend the simplicity of its accessibility, and rightly so. This understanding does not come through the power and wisdom of men (logic) but through the power and wisdom of God (1 Corinthians 1:18) by His Holy Spirit. For those who try to appropriate God's plan by any other means, this revelation will assuredly escape them, never manifesting until there is a complete surrender to God by acknowledging our sinful nature and need for the Saviour. Christ's wisdom then becomes our own (1 Corinthians 1:30) and He enables us to identify, respond and commit to the call of the Master.

Those things that we find to be self-empowering automatically receive our pledge of allegiance; our intellect, wealth, abilities, youthfulness, the list is exhaustive. While these resources are valuable assets that support our execution of the call of God, these strengths have no spiritual enablement in and of themselves; it only comes from the Holy Spirit. If we choose to yield the fullness of our existence to God's supernatural power, then the restrictions and limitations of human empowerment would become increasingly obvious. Indeed, through our submission we would certainly prize and treasure the godly strength we find in humility, and the spiritual values intentionally cast aside by our modern society in support of man's attempt to reach God on his terms, through works of the flesh. But, Paul makes it abundantly clear that no flesh can be acknowledged or congratulated for fulfilling the works of the Spirit.

Through our ever-increasing spiritual insight and godly wisdom, we would no longer see value in exchanging our weakness for the vainglory of self-sufficiency. It is only in Christ's sufficiency we are made self-sufficient, infusing us with inner strength and confident peace (Philippians 4:13), confirming that we do not need any outside help for in Him we are complete.

And in Him you have been made complete [achieving
spiritual stature through Christ], and He is the head over
all rule and authority [of every angelic and earthly power].
Colossians 2:10 (Amplified Bible)

 # Day 8

Day 34
Breaking Tradition

2 Thessalonians 2:13–15 (Amplified Bible)

[13]But we should and are [morally] obligated [as debtors] always to give thanks to God for you, believers beloved by the Lord, because God has chosen you from the beginning for salvation through the sanctifying work of the Spirit [that sets you apart for God's purpose] and by your faith in the truth [of God's word that leads you to spiritual maturity]. [14]It was to this end that He called you through our gospel [the good news of Jesus' death, burial, and resurrection], so that you may obtain and share in the glory of our Lord Jesus Christ. [15] So then, brothers and sisters, stand firm and hold [tightly] to the traditions which you were taught, whether by word of mouth or by letter from us.

WHETHER HANDED down by genealogy, culture or nationality, traditions have sentimental and sacred value that can define who we are. Our belief systems and behavioural patterns easily demarcate one family, clan, people group or country from another. From doctrines and laws to folklore, mind-sets and even diet, traditions passed from one generation to the next purport that their practice override all other similar approaches to being and living. Notwithstanding traditions may indeed serve their practitioners effectively, they can also be a source of fierce conflict with non-conformists, both within or outside of any given sect. Breaking free from them is not always the easiest task, and for anyone intent on absconding its bondage, the penalty can be as catastrophic as death.

In Jesus' day traditions had become so prevalent among the Pharisees that in some instances they were given the same honour as the Torah, their sacred law. In one such instance, the Pharisees used their traditions to challenge the disciples' practice regarding cleanliness and eating. Responding to their chagrin, Jesus pointed out that their tradition of using ceremonially clean hands to eat did nothing to purify their unclean hearts or make them righteous before God. He went on to explain to the disciples when they were alone that it is from within our hearts, our think-centre, that ignoble and sinful thoughts emerge and become sinful behaviour, uninfluenced by food whether eaten with clean or unclean hands (Mark 7:1–23).

If we expect the ceremonial and religious traditions of men or the law to sanctify us and make us righteous before God, then we would have effectively diffused the purpose and result of salvation through grace established in Jesus Christ. In fact, it would mean, therefore, that our sanctification and righteousness are received through our own efforts, by what we can do for ourselves. However, if our righteousness could be achieved via this means, the death of Christ would have no worth and He would have died for nothing (Galatians 2:21). But as Isaiah so rightly put it, all the righteousness of men adds up to a ball of filthy rags that diverts us far away from God's favour leading us towards our destruction (Isaiah 64:6). In essence, we have none and can create none on our own.

Foremost in Paul's writings is his awareness of being continuously indebted to God for the redemptive work of Christ in his life and his incessant thankfulness for all other recipients and partakers of this same grace. With the advent of the gospel and its sanctifying power to recreate us into the likeness of Jesus Christ by faith, he establishes through the work of the Holy Spirit that this new life cannot be sustained by our pre-Christ traditions and teachings; it is impossible. Instead, we are admonished to embrace and cling onto the revelation of our restored relationship with God. By accepting what He accomplished through His death, burial, and resurrection, we are enabled to achieve this goal and be established in our new position, seated in heavenly places with Christ (Ephesians 2:4–6) in a place of rest (Hebrews 4:11).

> **"...under this new covenant established in the finished work of Christ, we are called to become just like Him having understood His love for us."**

Paul also reinforces that under this new covenant established in the finished work of Christ, we are called to become just like Him having understood His love for us (1 John 4:17). We have an opportunity to obtain and share in His glory being made joint-heirs with Christ (Romans 8:17) by the spirit of adoption that grants us access to Abba Father (Ephesians 1:5). It was always God's plan for man to exist in an atmosphere saturated with His love, grace and peace and through Jesus we can be restored to this level of existence with Him. Jesus came to reconcile us to God and forever close the gap of spiritual death and eternal separation from God, our consequential inheritance from Adam's sin. Hence, we are no longer required to honour the irrelevant tradition of offering an insufficient animal sacrifice to God for our sin bondage, Jesus has it covered.

Today we are the recipients of Jesus' ultimate sacrifice by faith, fully justified and redeemed from sin, free to be the sons and daughters of the Most High God (2 Corinthians 6:18). If you haven't yet, I encourage you to start living by these new traditions that lavish on us the liberty and freedom of Christ and establish our right to come boldly before the throne of grace (Hebrews 4:16). There is no need to cling to the old ones that enslave us anymore, a new day and a new way have come.

In [this] freedom Christ has made us free [and
completely liberated us]; stand fast then, and do not be
hampered and held ensnared and submit again to a yoke
of slavery [which you have once put off].
Galatians 5:1 (Amplified Bible, Classic Edition)

Day 7

Day 35
Latter Redemption

Joshua 2:1 (Amplified Bible)

¹Joshua the son of Nun sent two men as scouts secretly from Shittim, saying, "Go, view the land, especially Jericho [the walled city]." So they went and came to the house of a prostitute named Rahab, and lodged there.

Matthew 1:2–6

²Abraham was the father of Isaac, Isaac the father of Jacob, Jacob the father of Judah and his brothers,

³Judah the father of Perez and Zerah, whose mother was Tamar, Perez the father of Hezron, Hezron the father of Aram,

⁴Aram the father of Aminadab, Aminadab the father of Nahshon, Nahshon the father of Salmon,

⁵Salmon the father of Boaz, whose mother was Rahab, Boaz the father of Obed, whose mother was Ruth, Obed the father of Jesse,

⁶Jesse the father of King David, King David the father of Solomon, whose mother had been the wife of Uriah,

*B*Y ALL SOCIAL standards Rahab must have been part of a disgraced faction in Jericho. Surely she was an outcast that was shunned, shamed and scorned for practicing '*the world's oldest profession*'. The odds that Joshua's scouts, representatives of the Most High God, would seek refuge in such a reprehensible literal hole in the wall may have been slim by the same standards. But then again, it might have been the obvious choice for the same reason. After all, who would take any particular interest in the goings-on at the domicile of their iniquitous hostess? Needless to say, the king still got wind of their presence and requisitioned their immediate release to the authorities of Jericho.

It is most interesting, however, that this contemptible, vile and immoral woman discerned the plan of God, stood against her own people and submitted to a call that would eventually absolve her sin and ultimately redeem her. It had been at least forty years since the unforgettable phenomenal Red Sea crossing she recounted during her plea, but the passing of four decades did not diminish their anxiety and distress. They lived in total fear of the God of Israel, and their day of reckoning had finally arrived. Rahab was acutely aware that Jericho's foreseeable future was hopelessly doomed but did not anticipate that God's favour would be extended to her, a common prostitute, and she would escape total annihilation.

Many times believers grapple with the culpability of past delinquencies and disreputable deeds, feeling helpless against their guilt and its continuous accusation as a memorial of their unworthiness of God's love. This stronghold drives a wedge between our confession of Christ and the affirmation of His redemption in our lives, although already ours when we accepted Him as Saviour. Some may believe that their regeneration is discredited and integrity overshadowed by the stain, wondering whether it is even possible to live totally redeemed of their past and complete in Christ. Well, the answer is yes, it is not only possible but it is encouraged, and it's yours.

It is true that God sees us as we are, weak and helpless in our sins that separate us from knowing His love and care as our Heavenly Father (Ephesians 2:12). It is equally true that once we receive sonship status by faith, the likeness of Jesus Christ instantly takes effect in us through grace (Galatians 4:7) whereby the stain of our sin, all our sin, is completely washed away (1 John 1:7–9). Being purified by God, our guilty conscience becomes a mere smokescreen that the enemy uses to keep our minds in bondage when we have already obtained and secured eternal redemption through the blood of Christ (Hebrews 9:12).

Rahab probably saw her request as a mad dash for survival, maybe even an opportunity to start afresh in a new place where her tainted past wasn't public knowledge. But even in her sinful state, God had purpose written all over her life. By her actions on this fateful day, this prostitute and social blemish was grafted into the most famous lineage in history through whom King David and Messiah, King of Kings would come. Today her name is immortalized in scripture as an example for the world to take note.

> **"...once we receive sonship status by faith, the likeness of Jesus Christ instantly takes effect in us through grace..."**

It is impossible for us to know how many people have been or will be affected by our answer to the call of the Master. The choice that Rahab made brought her salvation from her life of sin and ultimately redemption for our entire world. She chose to embrace God's purpose when she answered that knock at the door, not only to her home but also to her heart. She recognised and stood up for righteousness even in her unrighteous state and received a greater blessing than just survival, she received new life.

> Who [willingly] gave Himself [to be crucified] on our behalf to redeem us and purchase our freedom from all wickedness, and to purify for Himself a chosen and very special people to be His own possession, who are enthusiastic for doing what is good.
>
> **Titus 2:14 (Amplified Bible. Classic Edition)**

Day 6

Day 36
The Lord, Our Helper

1 Samuel 7:8–12 (Amplified Bible)

[7]Now when the Philistines heard that the Israelites had gathered at Mizpah, the lords (governors) of the Philistines went up against Israel. And when the Israelites heard it, they were afraid of the Philistines. [8]And the sons of Israel said to Samuel, "Do not cease to cry out to the Lord our God for us, so that He may save us from the hand of the Philistines." [9]So Samuel took a nursing lamb and offered it as a whole burnt offering to the Lord; and Samuel cried out to the Lord for Israel and the Lord answered him. [10]As Samuel was offering up the burnt offering, the Philistines approached for the battle against Israel. Then the Lord thundered with a great voice that day against the Philistines and threw them into confusion, and they were defeated and fled before Israel. [11]And the men of Israel came out of Mizpah and pursued the Philistines, and struck them down as far as [the territory] below Beth-car. [12]Then Samuel took a stone and set it between Mizpah and Shen, and he named it Ebenezer (stone of help), saying, "Thus far the Lord has helped us."

THROUGH A SERIES of events stemming from the unrepentant sins of Hophni and Phinehas and their lack of reverential fear for God in their Levitical calling, Israel whittled down to treating their most sacred emblem as a good luck charm for war. The Ark of the Covenant, symbolizing the eternal presence of God in Israel, was subsequently lost after their dismal defeat by the Philistines. In the aftermath, news of their downfall and the Ark's confiscation brought forth the declaration of Ichabod, the name given to Eli's grandchild, marking the departure of God's glory from Israel and the end of this priestly lineage (1 Samuel 4:21). It would be 20 years hence when the Ark would be returned to Israel during the reign of King David (2 Samuel 6:12–19).

During Samuel's early years in the temple, God called him one night and told him of a day to come when Eli's family would be destroyed as a consequence of sin (1 Samuel 3). While this day would be shrouded in destruction and despair at the hand of the Philistine army, there was another day appointed in Israel's future, a day of restoration when Israel would receive deliverance from the Philistines' era of tyranny. When the people pleaded with Samuel to seek God for divine intervention, his sacrifice was accepted and his supplication answered. Israel witnessed the unchanging omnipotence of God and received His supernatural enablement to defeat the Philistines. Through Samuel's continuous submission to the call of God, the nation was delivered from one of their most formidable adversaries.

> **God is the essence of second chances, providing every opportunity for His children to be restored, rooted in His matchless love and abounding grace.**

God is the essence of second chances, providing every opportunity for His children to be restored, rooted in His matchless love and abounding grace. What is most remarkable about God's scorekeeping is that somehow, regardless of the number of times we fail Him, a second chance to make things right always seems to come our way. Despite our insolent squirming, disregard, dissatisfaction, and rejection of His lordship when it opposes our desires, He's made every provision for our forgiveness and reconciliation while He awaits our trust and submission.

Undeniably, we are helpless against the attacks of the enemy if we commit to waging war in our physical, limited strength or carnally brandish the weapons and armoury of the Lord without understanding their purpose and power. We know as believers that in this battle, the work of darkness against us is strategic, clever and deliberate by design to ensure loss, destruction and death (John 10:10). Walking in victory would then require that we be discerning, applying spiritual insight that sharpens our awareness and ability to decipher the enemy's tactics. The resultant supernatural empowerment of the Holy Spirit equips to pull down, overthrow and destroy every evil scheme of our adversarial community as we bring every ungodly ideology captive to the obedience of Christ (2 Corinthians 10:5).

Whenever we feel the most vulnerable and susceptible to the enemy's attacks, we must remember that it is Almighty God who fights on our behalf (Exodus 14:13–14) and in Him, every battle is already won. We deny ourselves of receiving many victories and an overcomer's grace whenever we decide our way is better than God's, allowing our desires to override His plans. This self-serving approach is rooted in pride and robs us of the perfect rest that our humility and submission bring. Being embattled is not His plan for us, and only by His enablement would we receive the *"more than a conqueror"* status (Romans 8:37) that we have been called to enjoy. Let us then fight the good fight by faith with thanksgiving unto EBEN-EZER; The Lord Our Helper, who gives us His eternal pledge that through Him our victory is already guaranteed (1 Corinthians 15:57). He has helped us this far and He will help us to the very end.

Behold, God is my helper and ally;
The Lord is the sustainer of my soul [my upholder].
Psalm 54:4 (Amplified Bible)

Day 5

Day 37
Intercession In Instability

1 Samuel 30:3–8 (Amplified Bible)

³When David and his men came to the town, it was burned, and their wives and their sons and their daughters had been taken captive. ⁴Then David and the people who were with him raised their voices and wept until they were too exhausted to weep [any longer]. ⁵Now David's two wives had been captured, Ahinoam the Jezreelitess and Abigail the widow of Nabal the Carmelite. ⁶Further, David was greatly distressed because the people spoke of stoning him, for all of them were embittered, each man for his sons and daughters. But David felt strengthened and encouraged in the Lord his God.

⁷David said to Abiathar the priest, Ahimelech's son, "Please bring me the ephod." So Abiathar brought him the ephod. ⁸David inquired of the Lord, saying, "Shall I pursue this band [of raiders]? Will I overtake them?" And He answered him, "Pursue, for you will certainly overtake them, and you will certainly rescue [the captives]."

SHOCK, HEARTBREAK, grief and sorrow quickly transformed a group of faithful and devoted followers into a lynch mob. David's battalion of mighty men made him responsible, and therefore liable, for the devastation they met when they returned to Ziklag and the loss of all their loved ones. He was just as distraught as they all were having lost his wives in the raid also, but despite his emotional distress he had to find answers immediately for it seemed his very life depended on it.

But isn't that just like the enemy to attack you when your back is turned, when you least expect, when you are most vulnerable and where it will hurt you the most? And, isn't it also characteristic of the enemy to use a distressing situation to cause chaos in a once harmonious team, home, church, organization (you name it) to successfully bring division, discord and destruction? In times like these, we can become easily distracted from our true purpose by the intensifying distress encircling us. We may even question our calling and have great difficulty in seeing such a destructive situation as remotely resembling anything like the plan of God.

Let me categorically state that distressing attacks against the believer in Christ are not happenstance. The enemy's intent is to leave us broken, bewildered and destroyed by their effect. But, intrinsic to our faith in God who has called us with a holy calling (2 Timothy 1:9) is our ability to access godly strength and courage to make sound decisions in our most difficult battles that we must sometimes fight alone. This grace, however, cannot be found in simply performing rituals if we use David's example of putting on the ephod as part of our strategy. This action in and of itself has no power but it was his application of faith by his motive, intent and relationship with God that made all the difference.

> **66...intrinsic to our faith... is our ability to access godly strength and courage to make sound decisions in our most difficult battles...99**

The position David assumed as the priest was no self-serving move as some may believe because enquiring of the Lord was a priestly function on behalf of all Israel (Exodus 28:30; Numbers 27:21). While we could easily infer that the choice he made was to save his own life because his followers called for his head, the purpose and effect connote a greater sacrifice. As their leader, David sought God's will on behalf of everyone at a time when there was no one able to so do without malice or derision for their mutiny. He refused to be caught up in the emotional vortex enclosing on him with the potential to overpower his decision-making ability and instead he gave God His rightful place, sovereign over the call on his life regardless to the circumstances he faced.

Jesus Christ, the Anointed One and our High Priest has done the same for us. Even with our failures, challenges and despair churning all around us, He stands with us at the core, the very heart of our dilemma knowing our weaknesses and vulnerabilities intimately. By His grace we can freely access the help we need and receive His mercy with all confidence that His blessings will be ministered to us appropriately and continuously (Hebrews 4:14–16). Although we are diverse in our requests, He desires to meet everyone at the point of their specific and personal need.

Intercession during instability is not an easy call, but for the called, our submission in faith has a much greater effect than us keeling over in our distress. In so doing, we will find that the influence of external negatives gradually diminishes as we shift our focus to Him and His sovereignty in all things. The flailing of others that are in our same position is characteristic of a lack of trust in God's changeless omnipotence and absolute ability to deliver, which can be instantly dissolved by simply placing faith in Him. Be encouraged to seek the Father and trust His way, not only in times of suffering and sorrow, but always, even when everything seems to be on the up and up. God did not leave David *"hanging out to dry"* when he entreated Him for the immediate answers he needed that day and God will certainly never leave us to flounder in our urgent needs. What He did for David He most certainly will do for you and me, and we will never be disappointed for we too shall go up, overtake and recover all.

Inasmuch then as we [believers] have a great High Priest who has [already ascended and] passed through the heavens, Jesus the Son of God, let us hold fast our confession [of faith and cling tenaciously to our absolute trust in Him as Saviour].
Hebrews 4:16 (Amplified Bible)

 # Day 4

Day 38
Speak As God Speaks

1 Kings 22:10–14 (Amplified Bible)

[10]Now the king of Israel and Jehoshaphat king of Judah were each sitting on his throne, dressed in their [royal] robes, [in an open place] at the threshing floor at the entrance of the gate of Samaria; and all the prophets were prophesying before them. [11]Then Zedekiah the son of Chenaanah made for himself horns of iron and said, "Thus says the Lord: 'With these you will gore the Arameans (Syrians) until they are destroyed.'" [12]All the prophets were prophesying in the same way [to please Ahab], saying, "Go up to Ramoth-gilead and be successful, for the Lord will hand it over to the king." [13]Then the messenger who went to summon Micaiah said to him, "Listen carefully, the words of the prophets are unanimously favorable to the king. Please let your words be like the word of one of them, and speak favorably." [14]But Micaiah said, "As the Lord lives, I will speak what the Lord says to me."

*N*OBODY LIKES TO be the odd man out with the only opposing view. You make your contribution in the powwow, and the next thing you know you are branded as a weird trouble maker solely responsible for the hung jury experienced by all. Through narrowed eyes with furrowed brows, everyone looks at the misfit in the room who's thrown the monkey wrench in the gears of progress. Some may try to sway your vote, change your opinion or discredit your resolve to manipulate the result for their favour. How then do we mitigate such incidences and altogether represent truth and maintain our integrity?

King Ahab approached King Jehoshaphat and they both agreed to wage war against Syria for a plot of land belonging to Israel. In response to King Jehoshaphat's prompting, King Ahab called upon almost four hundred prophets to get confirmation from the Lord that war was the answer. When a 100 percent positive response was received, King Jehoshaphat's distrust led him to call for another prophet, or rather, any other prophet. Although King Ahab's proffered Micaiah whom he knew was not amongst the group of prophets that stood before them, he did this despairingly as this prophet was different. His prophecies never supported the king's decisions, proving that he was the resident maverick in their camp, but maybe he was the truth that King Ahab preferred to be silenced.

When we encounter people in authority who are only interested in God's directives on condition that it suits or supports their purposes, we are more challenged to tell them the truth in the wake of its sometimes deadly consequences. It gives us all great comfort when a bonafide prophet of God comes to town and sanctions our plans and future endeavours. However, it is only through humility can we surrender to His will when it takes us in a different and totally unexpected direction. For the sake of pride and arrogance, King Ahab missed the mark with God by Micaiah's words as he explained the deception of the prophets' unanimous refrain to attack Syria. As the king tried to silence the prophet through imprisonment, the time came when the word of the Lord spoken against King Ahab was fulfilled. He eventually paid the ultimate price for his hard-heartedness with his life.

Jesus made it abundantly clear that He only spoke what the Father told Him (John 12:49–50). Prior to Jesus' declaration, it was revealed that many leaders who heard Him believed but overwhelmed with the fear of being excommunicated and debarred from the synagogue by the Pharisees, they did not confess their faith in Him openly (John 12:42–43). It is common for the spirit of fear to creep in and brainwash us into believing that man's approval is more important than God's, especially when our declarations automatically generate sanctions against us in the places where we add value. There was nothing that stood between Micaiah

> **66 Whether we are required to sound an alarm, give words of encouragement or prophesy; our obedience to God is integral to the faith process. 99**

and the consensus to please the king except godly truth and a choice to make that truth public. Compelled by his commitment to the call of the Lord, he chose to speak truth knowing that it was going to cost him much, but this was insignificant when he considered God's commission and His expectation of him.

Whether we are required to sound an alarm, give words of encouragement or prophesy, our obedience to God is integral to the faith process. Being called upon to speak as He speaks and do as He instructs may seem costly when we see relationships change and friends walk away. Despite how difficult or unconventional our task may seem, we can find strength in the one who called us. In the face of human criticism, disapproval and contempt there is no wiggle room to alter the word of God to suit anyone's fanciful requests, ego or expectations. While it can be difficult to sometimes come to terms with what God requires of us, we must remain steadfast in performing the duty that God has entrusted in our care. He is counting on us to be His voice of clarity in the earth for the hearers to know that He is God, and beside Him, there is none other (Isaiah 45:5).

Truly life and death are in the power of our tongue and we will reap the results of the one we love more (Proverbs 18:21). We have the power to decide whose interest we will represent and whether we will save face or save lives. I can tell you, being the one singled out for the sake of truth and righteousness is never a bad thing. When we choose to mirror Christ, we will always honour God and embrace eternal life when we speak as He speaks.

[49]For I have never spoken on My own initiative or authority,
but the Father Himself who sent Me has given Me a
commandment regarding what to say and what to speak.
[50]I know that His commandment is eternal life. So the
things I speak, I speak [in accordance with His exact
instruction,] just as the Father has told Me."
John 12:49–50 (Amplified Bible)

 # Day 3

Day 39
Faith Beyond Our Failsafe

Job 1:8–12 (Amplified Bible)

⁸The Lord said to Satan, "Have you considered and reflected on My servant Job? For there is none like him on the earth, a blameless and upright man, one who fears God [with reverence] and abstains from and turns away from evil [because he honors God]." ⁹Then Satan answered the Lord, "Does Job fear God for nothing? ¹⁰Have You not put a hedge [of protection] around him and his house and all that he has, on every side? You have blessed the work of his hands [and conferred prosperity and happiness upon him], and his possessions have increased in the land. ¹¹But put forth Your hand now and touch (destroy) all that he has, and he will surely curse You to Your face." ¹²Then the Lord said to Satan, "Behold, all that Job has is in your power, only do not put your hand on the man himself."

Job 42:10

¹⁰The Lord restored the fortunes of Job when he prayed for his friends, and the Lord gave Job twice as much as he had before.

*J*OB WAS KNOWN throughout the land for his outstanding character, great wealth and reverence for God. His run-in with hard times was practically like a king being deposed based on the level of honour he had in the territory of northern Arabia. Above all his success, his fear for God sat at the pinnacle of his heart insofar that he regularly foraged the lives of his children for any evidence of sin or misconduct just for an excuse to atone everyone. He left no stone unturned regarding his hunger for righteousness before the Lord and remained devout to Him throughout his life.

It must have been earth-shattering to learn that his whole empire and worse, his entire lineage had been destroyed in a matter of moments, a legacy that took a lifetime to build gone in an instant. But his suffering didn't stop there. After being financially ruined and having his family wiped out, disease set in covering his entire body with boils. Well clearly the truth was now revealed about Job's secret life of sin that he had somehow successfully kept hidden from everyone. God was ready to judge and now Job had to pay big time while his remaining voice of comfort turned vengeful when his wife compelled him to "...*curse God and die!*" (Job 2:9) What could he hold on to, what witness remained of his exemplary unwavering commitment to his God, there was nothing left. Nothing but faith.

Many times we assume that sudden calamity and misfortune in our lives or the lives of other believers is a form of retribution, godly karma for our wrongdoing. Jesus had to confront this mental stronghold when He came upon a man who had been blind from birth as instinctively His disciples questioned the root of the sin that resulted in the blindness he suffered (John 9). Jesus' unexpected response dismantled this concept by removing the centre of attention from sin and placing it on the display of

God's glory that would come through his condition. Similarly, in Job's predicament, it is the manifestation of God's glory that would pierce the darkness that surrounded him and bring him victory.

We think of Job as being synonymous with patience, but for him, and us, it is the trial of our faith that brings us to this place of Christian maturity (James 1:2–3). As such, patience has become quite unpopular among all the virtues because we don't particularly care for the trials that unavoidably punctuates the journey. Job's faith gave him the courage to continue to stand in his darkest hour, albeit alone, trusting that God's ways were best. He bowed before God in continued reverence as he worshiped Him, believing in His supremacy even if the mountain of evidence said otherwise. He held on to God's will, trusting that it would be accomplished in his life, even if it would result in his death (Job 13:15). He saw his own weakness and frailty but Job's relentless faith in God throughout his ordeal kept him from allowing the single-most destructive entity from ever entering his heart and mind, doubt.

> **"...the life we are called to live is greater than the individual challenges that we go through and our God is bigger and greater than all of them combined."**

In death, loss and sickness it is possible for the deluge of grief and self-pity to overwhelm the best of us, and in this unstable emotional state, throwing in the towel could actually look like a step up. But the life we are called to live is greater than the individual challenges that we go through and our God is bigger and greater than all of them combined. Job's victorious end came through his unwavering faith in God who re-established his foundation, family, and fortunes surpassing the quality and quantity of his former dynasty. God's faithfulness to Job is not isolated but exemplifies His faithfulness to us as well. Through every storm, every valley and every attack of the enemy He watches over and protects us, loving us unconditionally. He is faithful who has called us to so great a salvation and, in the end, it is only Jehovah, our covenant-keeping Lord that truly has all power to save.

Faithful and absolutely trustworthy is He who is calling you [to Himself for your salvation], and He will do it [He will fulfill His call by making you holy, guarding you, watching over you, and protecting you as His own].
1 Thessalonians 5:24 (Amplified Bible)

 # Day 2

Day 40
Instructions For Life

Proverbs 3:1–6 (Amplified Bible)
[1]My son, do not forget my teaching,
But let your heart keep my commandments;
[2]For length of days and years of life [worth living]
And tranquility and prosperity [the wholeness of life's
blessings] they will add to you.
[3]Do not let mercy and kindness and truth leave you
[instead let these qualities define you];
Bind them [securely] around your neck,
Write them on the tablet of your heart.
[4]So find favor and high esteem in the sight of God and man.
[5]Trust in and rely confidently on the Lord with all your heart
And do not rely on your own insight or understanding.
[6]In all your ways know and acknowledge and recognize Him,
And He will make your paths straight and smooth [removing
obstacles that block your way].

*N*EW ACQUISITIONS always generate excitement,
bringing glints of enthusiasm to our eyes and giving
away our heightened anticipation to experience the *je
ne sais quoi* of something novel. However, wading through
instruction manuals isn't always high on our list of priorities,
even when the user stands to benefit from the knowledge to be
acquired therein. We'd rather just enjoy the experience at hand

minus the stress of diagrams on product assembly, optimization, safety, or instructions on how to troubleshoot problems should we encounter them.

For every believer, new instructions for life were made available to us when we accepted Jesus as our Saviour, guiding us along the path of our God-ordained purpose. It is possible, however, for us to receive Christ's salvation and still live outside of the grace provided for us to walk in the abundant life due to ignorance or resistance. It is all part of God's plan for us to share in His bountiful spiritual blessings and heavenly inheritance, walk daily in His new mercies and see His faithfulness in every situation. For us to receive the fullness of His glory in our lives, we must allow ourselves to be led by His instructions – intentionally, habitually and continually.

> **"For us to receive the fullness of His glory in our lives, we must allow ourselves to be led by His instructions – intentionally, habitually and continually."**

The guidance in this passage creates an enriching environment where we experience God's peace, favour and direction. It is easy to embrace these realities when the prevailing circumstances around us are favourable, but when we face turbulence in our daily lives, we may find it's not as simple as we first thought and even feel obligated to obey only under duress. Solomon advises that our lives be defined by godliness, recognizing that God's methods do not have to meet our standards because they are not so limited and astronomically beyond our insight. We are admonished primarily to obey His word, an action laden with benefits as He promises us a fulfilling and rewarding life with prosperity. However, it is when we receive the simplest of instructions that we sometimes falter. Our continued obedience to His directives, despite its superficial peculiarity, essentially gives us the key to unlock all of His riches and enjoy His choicest blessings.

We are also encouraged not to even make a move unless the Master directs us, acknowledging Him in everything we do and thereby receive instructions for the path are called to follow. We do not know what lies ahead unless God reveals it to us. He knows the pitfalls that we face daily and through our submission to His will, we are enabled to completely avoid them at times and go through tenaciously when necessary. Without His guidance, we become vulnerable to unscheduled detours, decelerating snares and deceptive entrapments that distract and divert us away from attaining our true goals.

We can all attest to the fact that commencing a journey is, in many instances, a lot easier than enduring the difficulties encountered along the way. The unexpected hurdles, the wearying challenges and the enemy's ambushment can cause even the strongest to succumb. Nonetheless, as we place our faith in the strength, power and might of Jehovah God, who called us to resist the urge to trust our own strength, we will encounter victory at every turn.

Let us understand today that the simple price we must pay to unleash all that God has in store for us, His beloved children, is our total submission. As such, let us view the struggles, though tough at times, as our opportunity to gain greater intimacy with

God. Let us see the vales that we pass through as a time to increase our dependence on His voice to lead us out as we focus on the light of His glory and grace. Let us give our insecurities and insufficiencies over to Him and in exchange receive His grace, enablement and abundance.

As we submit to the Master's call He takes charge of everything that the fulfilment of our purpose entails. We are therefore endowed from above with all that we need to triumphantly fulfil our destiny in Him. Hence, there is no need to fear the implications of saying yes to His call; He has already made provision for each journey. All that remains for us to do is to release our lives into the hands of El Shaddai and allow Him to be the Father that He has promised us He will be when we truly learn to let go and let God take absolute control. Purpose and destiny require our response, so resolve to give His presence a real opportunity in your life by saying *"Yes!"* to the call of Jesus, the one and only true Master, and live daily following His hand and fulfilling His plan. You will certainly never be disappointed at your journey's end because He will be right there waiting to embrace you, His beloved child.

And those whom He predestined, He also called;
and those whom He called, He also justified [declared
free of the guilt of sin]; and those whom He justified,
He also glorified [raising them to a heavenly dignity].
Romans 8:30 (Amplified Bible)

 # Day I

TO CONTACT
CHARA HOSEINEE-FRIDAY:

Email:
DeeperDevotionals@mail.com

Facebook:
https://www.facebook.com/Deeper Devotionals
Chara Hoseinee-Friday

Instagram:
charahfriday

Made in the USA
Columbia, SC
07 September 2022